PHILIP SERRELL

What Am I Bid?

HODDER

First published in Great Britain in 2021 by Hodder & Stoughton
An Hachette UK company

This paperback edition published in 2022

1

A CIP catalogue record for this title is
available from the British Library

Paperback ISBN 9781529396492
eBook ISBN 9781529396478

Typeset in Sabon by Hewer Text UK Ltd, Edinburgh
Printed and bound in Great Britain by Clays Ltd, Elcograf S.p.A.

Hodder & Stoughton policy is to use papers that are
natural, renewable and recyclable products and made
from wood grown in sustainable forests. The logging and
manufacturing processes are expected to conform to the
environmental regulations of the country of origin.

Hodder & Stoughton Ltd
Carmelite House
50 Victoria Embankment
London EC4Y 0DZ

www.hodder.co.uk

To Clem

Contents

Chapter 1

Old Mother Doings

I often get asked how someone who qualified as a PE teacher can end up being a scarf-wearing television auctioneer – truthfully the answer is with a boatload of luck. Part of that comes with the good fortune of having an employer who, nearly fifty years ago, had the time and patience to guide his young articled clerk.

It seems like yesterday when I had a job interview with a retired, pipe-smoking army major with a tin leg and a very vague memory. Mr Rayer – he had no time for military titles – was my first boss and was keen that I should follow him down the agricultural route. I had no experience of the type of business Mr Rayer was running – or any other business for that matter – so when he asked me to start on the agricultural side I didn't want to say no. I really needed the job , but a few unpleasant encounters with the wrong end of various farm animals soon taught me (and Mr Rayer) that I wasn't cut out for a life counting sheep. That's how I began my career in what was then the mysterious world of antiques.

It has been the best, if unorthodox, education and has taught me a lot of what I know. I now own a saleroom in the heart of rural Worcestershire and appear regularly on a number of antique programmes on the television. The stories in this book are based on the colourful people, odd places and bizarre objects I have met along the way. Some of these have been changed, altered or amalgamated, but I would thank them all for the experience. One of the bizarre objects I have not changed is the variety of dodgy cars that have been ever present and, back in the day, they were even dodgier.

I never thought I'd be so grateful to one for breaking down. Staggeringly, it seemed that Rosemary 'Albert' Hall was not completely put off by the experience of a walk home in the rain and there might be an inkling of a romance here. Albert worked for Lloyd and Gold, the auctioneers, valuers, estate agents and surveyors, who were about five doors up the High Street from where I worked. I had been trying to ingratiate myself with her for some time – and failing miserably.

As my mate Jim Johnson, who worked for them as an auctioneer, put it, 'Mate, you're punching so far above your weight, you're going to get yourself badly bruised if not battered.'

It was the late 1970s and I was an impecunious auctioneer making his way in the world with Bentley, Hobbs and Mytton, a long-established firm in Worcester dating back to the late eighteenth century. It was run by a number of partners, but I was answerable to the aforementioned Major Ernest Edward Foley Rayer, MBE, TD, FRICS, CAAV. Mr Rayer, Ted or EEFR – but never Major – was a lovely man with a tin leg and a wardrobe of scorched clothes resulting from numerous pipe-lighting incidents.

Many of these occurred whilst driving his car, an old Triumph 2000 automatic known throughout the county as Thunderbird 4. A trip with him was more terrifying than any ride in a theme park. Not a surprise really – a man with a tin leg trying to light his pipe whilst avoiding oncoming traffic in a narrow country lane was not the best way to settle the nerves of an anxious passenger.

I wandered into the office on a Monday morning feeling that the world was a good place and the Serrell star was in the ascendancy. As I was soon to discover, this is tempting fate on a massive scale, as something is bound to turn round and bite you on the backside.

Hinge and Bracket were the two secretaries working in the office; they each smoked two packets of Benson and Hedges a day, but drank lemon tea because it was good for you. Sadly, in later years the former had more of an effect than the latter, as they both succumbed to the 'Big C'. They saw it as part of their job description to take me under their collective wings, but when it came to my chances with Albert in the romance stakes, they were very much in the Jim Johnson camp.

After the demise of my car, I felt it was time to raise the possibility of having a company vehicle. Mr Rayer wasn't the man when it came to such things and I was directed to one of the other partners: J. Clifford Atkins. JCA was an interesting man, who had made a lot of money in North America dealing with commercial real estate and had come back to join the practice. He was about five feet four tall, with a huge handlebar moustache that was about five feet five wide. It was personal topiary on a whole new level and required a team of horticulturists to look after it; he reminded me of the splendidly moustachioed comedian Jimmy Edwards.

Cliff's taste in clothes and cars made Toad of Toad Hall seem shy and retiring, and they were a mirror image of his character. They were loud in the extreme and the fact that he was stone deaf, with a need to shout, did nothing to contradict this. I was somewhat anxious about discussing a company car with him; he genuinely believed that in any deal, fifty–fifty was sixty–forty in his favour.

'I've spoken to Mr Rayer and mentioned to him that a company car might be a good idea, considering the mileage I am now doing.'

The fact that I had arranged to see Albert the following Friday accentuated the need; another breakdown would not be good.

'OK, I'll have a look for something for you.'

I was taken aback, as a negotiation involving the spending of money to benefit others was not normally on his agenda. I walked back into the office with an ever-growing feeling of wellbeing. I should have known better.

'Philip, is your car completely off the road?' Mr Rayer asked.

I replied nervously in the affirmative, knowing that this might mean a trip with him somewhere.

'Well, you'd better go with Windy to see Old Mother Doings.'

This was not good. Windy was called Windy simply because every step he took resulted in flatulence. It was quite bizarre – if he stood still nothing happened, but with every step there was an emission. It was in pace with his steps; a slow march meant a slow, steady bop-bop-bop, whilst if he broke into a trot it was as if a machine gun was going off. Thankfully, there were none of the other effects one normally associates with such actions, as the air remained quite pure. Windy was oblivious to it all; goodness knows where he thought his nickname me from.

We walked out of the office to Windy's car, accompanied by his own personal percussion department. His car was something else. He had always coveted a Morris 1000 Traveller, but couldn't afford one. His compromise was an Austin 1100 that he had converted into a half-timbered variant by screwing timber roof-battens to the side, which he had then varnished.

Off we drove to Old Mother Doings. I still had no idea who she was or why I was going there. I should explain that 'Doings' could be a person, a place or an object in Mr Rayer's world – you only knew which after a passage of time; at least in this instance we knew it to be a female. Occasionally Gubbins would be substituted for Doings.

One thing I loved about my job then, and still do now, is driving through the Worcestershire countryside past farms and smallholdings similar to the one in which I grew up. As we headed west towards Herefordshire, I sat back in Windy's car and enjoyed the peace and the quiet.

After a time and seemingly in the middle of nowhere, Windy announced that we had arrived, as we disappeared down a long drive with a Victorian farmhouse in the distance. Having worked with Mr Rayer for many years, Windy had a sort of sixth sense when it came to directions. You never planned a route; you simply arrived at your destination almost by accident.

The silence was broken as we got out of the car and made our way to the front door; it might have been the old horse in the field nearby, but I'm pretty sure it was my travelling companion.

I still had no idea who Old Mother Doings was and before I could question Windy on the subject, she appeared – at least, I assumed it was her.

'Good Morning, Mr Rayer has asked me to call and see you,' I said.

'Oh, I was expecting someone from Mr Rayer,' came the reply.

'Mr Rayer sent me – my name's Philip,' I said, introducing myself.

'Ah, Mr Philips – you don't know Mr Rayer, do you?'

Then Windy took a pace with the inevitable consequence.

'Did you hear something, Mr Philips?' I was sinking fast here. 'Sounded like a small pop gun going off.'

There are times in your life when it's time to take stock; this was one of them, as I started questioning whether I'd done the right thing by giving up a career as a teacher. After what seemed like an eternity, I discovered that Old Mother Doings wanted to sell what she called 'the old jam cupboard' – but I still didn't know what her name was.

We walked into the kitchen and there was the most glorious housekeeper's cupboard dating to about 1770. The key thing about oak furniture is the colour, or patina, and this cupboard had it in bucketfuls: it was the colour of richly chewed toffee with a depth that seemed inches thick. It was one of the best I had ever seen, and had an arrangement of four panel doors to the top with four more doors below. I opened one of them and was met with a wall of jars; homemade jam of every variety on every shelf.

'What's it worth?' asked Old Mother Doings. 'Been invaluable for storing jam in, but my son and his family are moving in and his wife wants a new kitchen.'

Worth? That was indeed the $64,000 question. I stood there staring at the cupboard; it was a piece of furniture that I coveted – did then and, although tastes have changed somewhat, I still do today. The problem with valuation is maintaining objectivity without being influenced by subjectivity. Having said that, I worked on the theory that if I liked it then everyone else would; although this was occasionally a flawed argument.

'I think it should make four to six thousand pounds.'

I could hear myself saying it and I certainly convinced myself I was right. Old Mother Doings must have been impressed as well, because as we walked out through the door, all I could hear was her saying, 'That's more than I expected – I'll get my son to drop it off.'

Well, that was easy enough, I thought. I just hoped I hadn't overvalued it – and I still didn't know her name.

Back in the office, I turned my thoughts to my date with Albert and exactly what sort of car I could persuade the firm to get for me. What would be really cool would be a sporty little number befitting my image as a young, trendy man-about-town. Perhaps an Italian job – a Lancia or an Alfa Romeo, I was fantasising to myself – how could Albert possibly fail to be impressed?

My gazing out of the window was rudely interrupted by Cliff Atkins wandering into my office, muttering, 'Right, right, jolly good.' These were words that bore no relevance to anything, but were Cliff's preamble to anything he was about to say.

'Your new car's outside, Philip.'

I was really impressed. Cliff, as good as his word, had bought me a car.

I think the word 'new' meant new-to-me, rather than brand-new, straight-out-of-the-box type new. I walked outside the rear office door to the car park wondering whether it was the Alfa or the Lancia. It was neither.

It was a green Fiat 500.

You couldn't argue about its country of origin; it was definitely Italian, but not quite from the stable I'd imagined. My father had bought me a green car some time back and I think that lasted a matter of days. Ah well, beggars can't be choosers; I thought I had better show good grace. All I could hear behind me was, 'Right, right, jolly good,' as I opened the car door.

I know I'm never going to appear in a slimming campaign, but I didn't know whether to sit in it or wear it.

'Should prove pretty economical, right, right?' said Cliff, who had joined me in the car park. 'I gave Brian Malting five hundred quid for it.'

My immediate reaction was that he had been robbed; Brian Malting was one of Cliff's drinking mates and his one financial weakness was with his pub cronies. I was doomed. It looked as if I was lumbered with the car and I didn't want to look a gift horse completely in the mouth – though a horse might have been a better option than the 'Green Thing'.

I started it up and listened to the strange noise as its two cylinders tried to reacquaint themselves with one another. As the engine began to warm up, the water temperature rose and the oil pressure dropped. Cliff told me that there were bound to be a few minor glitches, but once I'd run it for a week or so he'd get Bill Vicars, his trusted mechanic, to have a look at it. My heart was now down around my boots somewhere – Bill's toolkit comprised a bloody great hammer for the mechanicals and a four-inch paintbrush for the resprays.

As Cliff walked back into the office, muttering, 'Right, right, jolly good,' I sat there thinking this was neither right nor jolly good; this was not at all what I had planned. (In later years, whilst filming *Antiques Road Trip*, I was presented with another Fiat 500 as 'the car' for our journey. Time had not improved it.)

I decided to drive home early – certainly before Jim Johnson might see me in it. The car appeared to drive all right, but there was an overpowering smell of hot oil. The fuel gauge hardly moved as I drove back to my parents' smallholding. Cliff's words about being 'pretty economical' rang in my ears; this thing would run for a month on a cup of fuel, though I was a bit concerned at the oil pressure, which seemed to be dropping at a quicker rate than the sales of sand in the Sahara.

I pulled into the yard at my parents' place and my father simply stared at me. He wasn't known for being a great smiler, but a grin appeared on his face that I hadn't seen since my mother threatened to leave him fifteen years earlier.

'What the hell is that? You'll need a team of surgeons to get you out of it.'

I decided the best course of action was to ignore him. I thought I'd better give the Green Thing a onceover. The fuel gauge had not moved at all, so that was good; the temperature gauge appeared to be hovering where it should be, which was also good; the only fly in the ointment was the oil pressure gauge that flickered between about two and six pounds per square inch. Perhaps that's what these two-cylinder things did while ticking over – when it had all cooled, I would check the oil. The one upshot was that the bloody thing was so small, my date with Albert would most definitely be cosy. As I sat there daydreaming, I was awoken by my father calling me in for supper.

Supper wasn't a term my parents used to be up-market. Their daily food intake was as follows: 7 a.m. – breakfast; 11 a.m. – lunch; 1.30 p.m. – dinner; 4 p.m. – tea; and 7 p.m. – supper. All very confusing. It was a good job they never invited anyone around for dinner: the guests would arrive at

7 p.m. for a meal my parents had eaten five and a half hours earlier.

My mother was an advocate of Spam or cold meat, chutney and Smash – the instant mashed potato – which is fine now and then, but night after night was a bit wearing. Food with my parents was an intake of fuel, rather than a culinary delight.

It was time to check my new steed now it had all cooled down. I turned on the ignition and the fuel gauge was registering full, the radiator was full to the brim, but when I checked the oil the dipstick was as dry as a bone. On my parents' farm there was always oil and stuff in the sheds, so I mooched some and filled the oil tank up to the top. Clearly Brian Malting hadn't been too diligent when it came to maintenance; still, all sorted now.

Travelling to work was always a pain. Worcester is a city divided by the River Severn with one central bridge, resulting in traffic jams at both ends of the working day. I set off in the Fiat and was beginning to wonder if the dials were broken: the fuel gauge still hadn't moved at all, whilst the oil pressure gauge refused to budge from zero.

When I pulled into the office and climbed out of the cockpit – it was about the size of a cockpit in a small, single-seat plane – there was still a very strong smell of hot oil. Up came the bonnet; the dipstick was bone dry again and almost white hot at the end. I was no mechanic, but this was most definitely not right. Off I went to buy some oil from the nearby garage.

It was auction day and Old Mother Doings' jam cupboard was due to be sold. I was a little bothered about my four-to-six thousand guesstimate, but Mr Rayer came out with his usual, philosophical, 'What will be, will be, Philip.' That's all very well, but for someone who was making his way in the world, it was rather more important than that.

The jam cupboard had created quite a bit of interest during the viewing before the sale started, though I gleaned nothing from the dealers who I thought might be keen to put their hand up to bid on it. Cliff Atkins had the job of selling the cupboard; I had a huge amount of personal pride resting on this and I was sitting next to him on the rostrum, clerking the sale.

'Right, right. Lot 47 . . . jolly good . . . a fine old cupboard. Bid me.' There was the customary silence as the assembled throng looked at their shoes.

'A thousand, sir!' shouted a lone voice from the back of the room. This was some way off the four to six thousand I had quoted. I needn't have worried – going up in £50 bids, the hammer fell at £5,400, nearly at the top end of my estimate. I felt suitably pleased and proud of myself; it was a good piece of English country furniture and I had pretty much got it bang on. Nothing else came close to that price; by lunchtime it was all over, with dealers paying for and collecting their lots, and with curious vendors ringing to see what their family heirlooms had made.

'It's for you, Philip. Old Mother Doings wants to know what her cupboard made,' Mr Rayer shouted across the clerk's office to me. I picked up the phone with a smug self-satisfied look on my face.

'Well, it was a very good sale and your cupboard dresser sold for £5,400 – we're very pleased.'

It was blatantly obvious that Old Mother Doings was somewhat less than pleased, as she screamed down the phone to me, 'You told me it would make forty-six thousand pounds!'

I was almost speechless.

'I said it would make four to six thousand pounds.'

'Yes . . . forty-six thousand pounds!'

I really didn't know what to say. It had sold well at £5,400 – and £46,000 was simply not possible for such a piece of furniture. Mr Rayer could see I was in some difficulty and took the phone from me, gently explaining the situation to her. I spent the rest of the day hiding from the saleroom porters, who were keen to have a laugh at my expense.

As I drove home that evening, I mulled over the whole saga – I don't think I've ever used the four-to-six thousand estimate since. And I still didn't know what Old Mother Doings' name was.

Then the oil light came on in the Green Thing, the smell of burning oil returned, and the oil pressure gauge registered zero. At this point, I considered telling Albert that our red hot date might be better put off for a while.

It was Friday evening and the night of the big date. Checking the oil in the Green Thing had become a full-time occupation and, sure enough, the dipstick appeared to be dry again. It was using more oil than petrol and I could see why the Getty family had made so much money out of liquid gold; most of it was used by owners of Green Things. Still, as long as it got me through this evening, all would be good. I topped it up from my now well-stocked reserve supply of Castrol and went in to get changed.

Suitably attired in my very best corduroy trousers and local farmer's store check shirt, I thought I cut quite a dash. I thought I would call into the Greyhound, our local pub, and see if Jim Johnson was there to offer a few pearls of wisdom, as well as get a pork pie and a pint; I hadn't quite got the appetite for my mother's Smash, chutney and cold meat.

I pulled into the pub car park and saw that Jim was already parked up. Trying to look cool getting out of the Green Thing was a challenge and, if I'm honest, I didn't pull it off. This was confirmed as I walked into the bar to be greeted by Jim, 'Bloody hell – have you just stepped out of a cheap clothes ad in the *Farmers Weekly*?', which he followed up with, 'Can the rest of you smell burning oil?'

I decided the best course was to ignore all this cheap talk and order a pie and a pint.

'What the hell are you doing? You can't go on a date with Albert stinking of booze. Get him an orange juice!'

Pork pie and orange juice didn't have quite the same ring to it, but I could see his point.

'And make sure that bloody oil burner doesn't conk out on you – breaking down on her twice would not be good news.'

He was absolutely right again, so I decided to make short work of the pie, leave the orange juice and set off. It wasn't so much that I wanted to warm the car up, but let it cool down. I drove the six or seven miles to Keane House where Albert lived with her parents, mentally going over the evening, and thinking of all the pitfalls and disasters that might happen.

I pulled gingerly into the drive of Keane House and parked the Green Thing next to a gleaming Aston Martin; which I knew was Albert's father's car. I knocked on the door, to be greeted by Mrs Hall.

'Ah, Philip, Rosemary's getting changed – do come in,' she ushered me into the drawing room. 'Sit down and you can have a chat with my husband.'

This was going to be fun. He was sitting in the corner, gin and tonic on the table by his side, smoking a Peter Stuyvesant cigarette and reading *The Times*, a broadsheet in those days, which hung in front of his face like a curtain round the coffin in a crematorium.

He didn't say much – in fact, he didn't say anything. I tried to engage him in conversation, but it was a one-way street; whatever I said or asked resulted in monosyllabic replies. The paper didn't move, remaining between us like a theatre safety curtain. 'Yes', 'No', 'Yes' replies to my manic attempts at making conversation resulted in me spouting even more gibberish. I became aware of what it meant to be in a cold sweat as beads of perspiration formed on my brow, whilst my hands took on a chill that made frostbite a possibility.

I decided the best course of action was to say nothing and let Mr Hall lead the conversation. Perhaps I should have let him in on my master plan, because the ensuing silence was deafening. He said nothing.

Eventually Albert walked in with a winning smile and I bade her father farewell as I shot through the door. I'm not sure if he replied – if he did, it was with a grunt – or whether he was simply clearing his throat; either way I was out of there.

Albert and I walked through the front door and she saw the Green Thing.

'It does look . . .,' I waited to hear what was coming next, 'sweet.'

I wasn't sure if she was extracting the Michael, but I thought it wasn't in her nature to do that. I smiled and opened the door, and she folded herself into Italy's revenge. We set off down the road and as we chatted about Old Mother Doings' jam cupboard, my anxiety levels started to rise, whilst the oil pressure began to fall.

'It's warm, isn't it?'

Warm didn't come close – it was like a sauna – and the smell of burning oil got stronger. Tactics were required and I decided to head to the nearest pub for a 'quiet drink', working on the theory that the fewer miles I drove, the lesser risk of another breakdown.

We had a really lovely evening, chatting about work, hobbies and the like. Turned out she was a real petrol head – I was going to ask her if she knew how to rebuild an Italian two-stroke, but thought I might be pushing my luck. We walked out to the car and I felt much more relaxed and chilled as we drove back to Keane House. We were about 500 yards from our destination when the Green Thing gave a little cough. I hoped it was just clearing its throat, but as we ground to a halt, it was clear it had expired its last breath. Bugger.

Albert started to laugh and I thought that was the end of that, until I cottoned on that she was laughing with me not at me. I walked her the short distance to her home and it occurred to me that broken-down cars might actually be the making of this relationship.

'I could always get my father to come and help?'

This was not an option as far as I was concerned. The last thing I wanted was a monosyllabic, Aston Martin-driving father grunting at me, my car, and my ineptitude in making it run. I was sure Albert's father was the type of man who placed a great deal of store in knowing the workings of the internal combustion engine.

'I'll soon have it running,' I lied. 'Let's get you home first.'

I walked her to the front door of her parents' house and beat a very hasty retreat before she could ask her father for help. I got back to my very own personal scrapheap challenge and thought if I let it cool down, it might get me home.

I wound the starter motor up and eventually it responded with the small car engine equivalent of an asthma attack. The journey home convinced me that prayer really does pay dividends, because I prayed every yard of the trip.

The next morning I telephoned the office to let them know that the Green Thing was terminally ill, and I was going to leave it at my parents' house and hitch a lift into Worcester.

I was expecting to be on the receiving end of strong words from JCA, but I think even he realised that his choice of car was not really appropriate.

'That little car probably wasn't suited to the mileage you were doing.'

This was a bit rich, seeing as I hadn't done many journeys at all, and not one over twenty miles.

'I'll get something a bit more suitable for you, Philip.'

I felt this might be some form of progress but, in the back of my mind, I knew I was dealing with a man who struggled to remember the combination to his wallet when it came to spending money on someone other than himself.

I was right.

Chapter 2

Mr Smith and Mr Smith

The next car chosen for me was a light blue Citroën 2CV with a canvas roof and lime-green seats.

'This should be better for you, Philip – good oil pressure and it's only done 30,000 miles.' And 25,000 of those were on the back of an AA Recovery truck, I thought to myself.

I knew there was no point in debating the new car. I was reasonably happy that Albert would be fine about it. Jim Johnson, however, was a different kettle of fish; he wouldn't be able to help himself from ripping into me at every opportunity. I could hear him now: 'Be ideal in Malvern that – they'll think you're a new age traveller heading for the common.'

I retreated to my office upstairs and took time to lie low. I decided to take the bull by the horns and give Albert a call; break it to her gently about my new steed. I phoned Lloyd and Gold and got straight through to her and we chatted away until it was time to bite the bullet.

'Fancy risking another drink at the weekend?' was met with, 'Yes, that would be lovely.' I was beginning to think we might be an item. It was time to break the news.

'I've got another car.'

Silence – followed by, 'What is it?'

'A Citroën.'

More silence. Perhaps we might not be an item after all. Then she replied, 'I quite like those little deux chevaux cars . . . look, I'm sorry, I've got to go. A client has come in.'

I don't think she was just being kind.

I spent the afternoon shuffling papers in my office until going home time, when I made my way down the stairs past Mr Rayer's room to the front reception office.

'Ah, Philip!' he shouted. It was more of a bellow really and I'm not even sure how he knew it was me. He must have had a sixth sense; everyone knew you had to creep past his office to avoid the bellow.

'On your way in tomorrow morning, I want you to call in to see the Doings. They've got some things they want valued.'

It was time for me to be assertive; normally I would have left and tried to work out where I was supposed to be going.

'Mr Rayer, who exactly are the Doings?'

This was new territory for Mr Rayer, as nobody had ever asked him such a question. 'For Lord's sake, Philip; the Doings from out Himbleton way – but they've moved now.'

Well, that was crystal clear. I shut the door and made my way to the reception, where Hinge and Bracket, the two office secretaries, eventually got the Doings' proper name and an address. Apparently the client was a Mr Wenlock, who now lived in Monmouth. How could I have failed to work that one out from him telling me about Doings and Himbleton?

I walked out to the car park and opened the door. I think it fair to say that the Citroën 2CV did not have the same sturdy appeal that it's German equivalent might have had. The bodywork resembled one of those aeroplane models we made as children out of balsa wood and tissue paper. It appeared to have its own crumple zone every time you leant on it.

I sat in the driver's seat, which was really an extension of the passenger's seat: a kind of bench seat deckchair. I put the key in the ignition and started it up. I've often heard about an engine that whines, but that's exactly what this thing did; a high-pitched noise that reached ever higher notes until it fired into life. On reflection, fire might be too strong a term; smoulder would be more accurate. The next issue was to work out the gear lever, which extended from underneath the dashboard like a gentleman's umbrella. Selecting a gear was like trying to stir porridge with a stick of rhubarb; it was one of life's lotteries.

I set off the next morning to the address I had for the Wenlocks, which was one of the new developments on the outskirts of Monmouth. I arrived at one of those modern Georgian-style, four-bed detached houses surrounded by other similar houses; the only difference from one to the next being the colour of the front door.

I knocked on the red door of this house to be met by Mr Wenlock, who was about sixty and very smartly dressed. He explained that his great-aunt had died and whilst the family had distributed all of her smaller items, the furniture from her small flat was scattered throughout his home. As we wandered round the ground floor, it became obvious that Great-aunt So-and-So was a collector of fairly ordinary, nineteenth-century mahogany furniture. There were corner cupboards, cabinets and sweet little side tables that were saleable, but would only be classed as saleroom fillers, or fodder, and might make between £200 and £500 per item.

'There's just one more item in the small bedroom upstairs,' Mr Wenlock said, as he led me along the hall and up the stairs. Small didn't come into it – this room was no larger than what my mother referred to as the 'smallest room in the house', which she thought was a very posh term. Sometimes I was convinced my mother was the role model for Hyacinth Bouquet in the TV series *Keeping Up Appearances*.

I'm sure when the estate agents sold the house, they described this as the fourth bedroom, but it was miniscule. There was a half-width single bed pushed up against the far wall and what appeared to be a chest and a display cabinet on the floor jammed next to it, both with an old sheet over them.

I took the sheet off and saw the most wonderful bureau, with a glazed cabinet by the side of it that would have sat on top to make a bureau bookcase. They were eighteenth-century and altogether a different kettle of fish from everything else I had seen.

The bureau had a flap that dropped down to reveal a fitted interior that was stepped, had an arrangement of pigeon holes and drawers, and a cupboard with a number of secret compartments. Below the flap were two short drawers and three long ones, and the whole thing was lifted off the floor by wonderfully shaped bracket feet. On top of the bureau sat the glazed bookcase, with glass doors that had fine glazing bars and opened to reveal a series of adjustable shelves.

All sounds pretty standard stuff, but it had a number of things going for it. The bureau section and the bookcase were both finely inlaid with cut brass lines and stars; the mahogany was the finest quality timber and to my eye looked as if it had never been touched other than polished – the colour was to die for; and the whole thing reeked of quality. I thought the brass inlay was very fine and striking and it was clearly designed by someone with an eye. The drawer handles and escutcheons were all finely cast and better than anything I had seen on a piece of furniture before. If Rolls-Royce had ever made a bureau bookcase, this was it.

'What do you think?' I could hear Mr Wenlock asking. It was an excellent question to which I wasn't sure I had the answer; I knew it was a good thing and someone with a greater knowledge than mine might have been able to put a name to the man who designed it.

I stood there looking at it; sooner or later, I was going to have to come up with a figure for auction. It might have come from a grand country house, that word 'provenance' is key in our business, but when I asked Mr Wenlock what he knew about it, the answer was a big fat zero. Valuation is about comparison of prices for similar objects, but I had seen nothing like this. I reasoned that if a good bureau bookcase made between £5,000 and £10,000 – and this was far better than one of those – then this one should make considerably more. It was decision time.

'It's difficult, as I haven't seen anything quite like it before, and if you decide to put it into auction I would like to try and do a little research. I think it's worth in the order of £20,000 to £30,000.'

It's very disconcerting when you wait for a reaction and there isn't one. We walked down the stairs and as he opened the front door for me to leave, all I got was, 'Thank you very much, Mr Serrell. My wife and I will have a think and come back to you.'

I walked back to my car unsure as to how I should be feeling. It wasn't coming in for sale at the moment, but it might, and I wasn't sure whether my figure was right or wrong, or Mr Wenlock thought it was right or wrong. It was all up in the air without a conclusive decision, which was frustrating.

It would have been a result to get it in for sale; not only for the financial reward, but also to try and find out more about it and, importantly, to confirm if my valuation was correct.

This was going to be one of those questions that might never have an answer. But – and it was a big but – it was one of the best bits of furniture I had seen. It was a piece that talked to you.

The Citroën wasn't that bad a car, though it probably wasn't a good one either. The gear lever, or stick, threw me into a bit of confusion, in that I was never sure which gear I was selecting. It made driving a voyage of discovery: not knowing whether you were going to set off in a forward or backward direction could make life quite exciting. I decided to park up and pull back the folding canvas roof and enjoy the sunshine. I closed my eyes and, ignoring the paper-thin bodywork and an engine note of a 45 rpm record being played at 78 rpm, with a bit of artistic licence you could imagine you were in ritzy sportscar. (Make that a lot of artistic licence.) Then you opened your eyes and reality soon returned.

My next appointment was to look at something I was more familiar with – Royal Worcester porcelain. The address I had was in Worcester, but the location did not ring any bells, though I knew roughly it was on the edge of a growing industrial area on the north side of the city. It was time to ask. I pulled up at a unit that had huge machines bending great big lumps of metal and gave the fork-lift truck driver the address I needed. He gave me some clear directions, but followed these up with 'Good luck', which I didn't quite understand but, hey-ho, ours is not to reason why and all that.

His parting remark became apparent as I drove into a travellers' caravan park with caravans and Ford Transit pick-up trucks of every size and colour. Now I have to say that travellers don't always get the best press, but the ones that I have dealt with through the years have always stuck to their words and been quite straightforward in their dealings. I think that if you treat people properly, they will respond in a positive manner.

Each pitch was numbered and I pulled up outside the one for my appointment. The Citroën looked slightly out of place as I parked next to a brand new, white BMW convertible and a six-month-old, top-of-the-range Mercedes, also in white. I knocked on the door of the caravan, which was in reality a spacious mobile home; I was thinking that bedroom four in this was probably bigger than that of the Wenlocks. As I walked in, I could see that the whole place was immaculate; you could have had a four-course meal off the floor and I've no doubt it would have been cleaned between each course.

What I do know about travellers' caravans is that they can house fabulous collections of twentieth-century English porcelain in general, and Royal Worcester porcelain and Royal Crown Derby in particular. As I made my way into the reception area, this was no exception. There were pots of all shapes and sizes in a purpose-built mahogany display cabinet.

'D'you like me vazes and me Durby?'

The Worcester collection was mainly vases that were hand-painted with rich fruit designs – although I was aware in my client's eyes they were 'vazes' not 'varses'. The Derby was Imari patterned – a rich blue-and-red design – and similarly was 'Durby' not' Darby'. There was tens of thousands of pounds worth here and unlike the Wenlocks' bureau, I was on secure ground in that I knew what I was talking about.

'We'd like to sell them pair o' Wuster vazes,' my new client told me, pointing to a pair of large and slender vases that were about forty years old and smothered with apples, peaches, pears and berries of all shapes and sizes, with a background of brightly burnished acid gilt. 'We was hoping we'd get about eight or nine thousan' fer 'em.'

I think this was more of a statement than a question as to what I thought they might be worth; as it happened, I think they were spot on with their valuation.

'Would yer like to tek 'em 'n sell em?'

This was music to my ears and I made my way out to my car to get a receipt book. As I opened the door to get outside, I saw that a fairly large crowd had gathered around the Citroën and most of them were between about eight and twelve years of age.

'Is this yer car, mister?'

I could tell this was not going to be a prelude to compliments, as the youngster behind the question was struggling to hold in fits of laughter.

'Is it fer a dare, mister?'

It was good-natured banter, but given that there was one of me and about fifteen of them, I decided I was horribly outnumbered. I made my way back inside without passing comment – other than giving them what I hoped was a disarming smile.

Mr Smith, that really was his name, had the pair of vases out of the cabinet with a large cardboard box and about four tons of old newspapers. I looked at them, made sure they were perfect and packed them away, leaving me to go through the paperwork with the Smiths. I noticed Mr Smith was getting a bit fidgety as I started to go through the form; documentation was clearly not his strong point.

'You tek 'em, sor – I've no need of yer paperwork – I trusts yer.'

I told him it would be a good idea if he read through the sale terms and conditions. This led to a considerable amount of more fidgeting followed by, 'I canner read,' and after a short pause, 'nor writ.' I don't know why, but I felt very uncomfortable at having put him in a position that he felt so awkward about. I explained to him the basics of the contract he was about to enter into, and he was happy to sign with a squiggle that I supposed was his mark.

I packed up the vases, making sure that there was a ton of paper around them, and went outside to the car and put them on the floor of the passenger's footwell. Mr Rayer, being something of a sage when it came to advice, always told me that if you put something on the floor, it couldn't fall any further; advice that I have carried with me until this day.

As I made my way back to the saleroom, I reflected on the difference between the two clients I had just seen. Then something dawned on me – why on earth did the Smiths have newspapers if they couldn't read? That was a question that I couldn't fathom the answer to, but my mind was quickly elsewhere as I went round a left-hand bend that was a little bit sharper than I first thought.

In a 'normal' car, this wouldn't have been an issue, but the Citroën rolled over to about 45 degrees. I decided the best course of action was to drive through it. I was to learn that this was very much the driving style to adopt as the '2CV roll' was a trait of these cars; it was nonetheless perfectly safe in its own very unsafe way.

I arrived at the saleroom, which was an old church hall in Malvern, and took the vases in. Windy was on duty; he unpacked them and put them into a display cabinet. An operation that required little movement and thus the attendant 'bottom burping' (this was another expression of my mother's that she thought sounded 'posh') was kept to a minimum. It was now mid-morning and I was at a loose end, so I decided to go back to the Worcester office and wander past Albert's office on the off chance that she was around for a lunchtime drink.

Trying to look nonchalant has never been a strong point, but I gave it my best shot as I wandered slowly past the offices of Lloyd and Gold, peering at the properties for sale in the window. I could see Albert behind a typewriter and eventually she looked up and I caught her eye. I wandered in and suggested, as it was now nearly lunchtime, we walk up to one of the pubs in town and grab a bite to eat. In those days Worcester was known for having a racecourse, making pots and sauce, and playing cricket; this particular pub was the haunt of some of the county cricket players.

I have always been a great cricket fan and as we walked in, the first person I saw was one of my heroes, the great all-rounder Basil D'Oliveira. Basil was a very humble man, who achieved greatness on the field – and off it with his dignity in the 'D'Oliveira Affair', when he was barred from an England Test tour in 1968–69 of his native South Africa during the apartheid era. Bars and Basil seemed to go very well together. (In later years I got to know the family well and this observation was confirmed on more than one occasion to my detriment.)

Albert and I ordered a sandwich each and shared a bottle of tonic water.

'What shall we do this weekend?' she asked.

I thought this was a huge step forward as it seemed to imply we were now an item, which was fine by me. We sat and chatted about where we might go and what we might do. I was acutely aware that funds were pretty tight for me, so any social planning had to be on a budget. Then she suggested, 'What about a drive out in the afternoon – I'll plan some-where – and a drink on the way home?'

Well, that all seemed good to me – it was almost what grown-ups did. We walked back to our respective offices and after work I decided to call into the Greyhound for a quick drink before the inevitable Spam/Smash combo. I had toyed with the idea of buying my mother a cookery book, but remembered that this was the woman who once cut the pink bits out of a Battenberg cake and covered them in a pink custard with the consistency of quicksand. Ordinarily you would have said it looked worse than it tasted, but this was most definitely not the case.

I pulled into the Greyhound car park. I was beginning to get the hang of the Citroën 2CV; it really did lean into corners at about 45 degrees and I had learned not to fight it. I parked up and went inside, waiting for Jim after ordering half a pint. This was partly out of deference to the drink-drive laws and partly out of budgetary constraints. I hadn't mentioned to Jim anything about my new car, but there was clearly no need as he stormed through the bar door.

'Bloody hell, is that your blue thing outside – has it got as many reverse gears as well as forward?'

The back end of this remark was really in poor taste and was a reference to France's involvement in the Second World War. Jim thought it was hilarious and insisted we went for a test drive. I tried hard to dissuade him, but he was having none of it as he ushered me out into the car park, muttering comments along the lines of 'General de Gaulle's staff car'.

As we got in, Jim shouted to me, 'Open her up then!'

I already had – an out-and-out sprint between this and the Green Thing would have been a close-run race, with France probably shading it over Italy. As we went around a left-hand bend at about 35–40 mph, I could feel the start of the 'lean' and I leant with it. This was not a problem for me, but it was not a technique that I had passed on to Jim. He reckoned he was a trim fifteen-and-a-half stone, whereas in reality he was a not-so-trim seventeen-and-a-half stone.

As we lurched around the bend like a circus clown's car, the customary angular lean took over and I looked up momentarily to see Jim appear about three feet higher than me, as the bench seat was now 45 degrees to the road. I'm not sure how they test seat belts in France, but clearly not with the stress of having a seventeen-and-a-half stone auctioneer stretching them to the limit. There was a low-pitched twang as if the string on a double bass was breaking. This was followed by Jim dropping down the seat and onto my lap as he screamed, 'Bugger me!' This was not helpful and did not make the whole driving process easier.

Eventually the Citroën fell back on an even keel and we made our way back to the Greyhound car park in silence. I had never known Jim so quiet – it's amazing what fear can do. As we parked up and got out, Jim turned round and said, 'Just don't tell me you're taking Albert out in that bloody thing – you're trying to date her, not kill her.' With some smug self-satisfaction, I told him we were off on a mystery road trip on Saturday.

I went back home for some food, wondering what culinary delights my mother had dreamt up for us tonight. It was *Spam Spaghetti à la Serrell*. She said she was trying to make her cooking more interesting. She had certainly achieved this, but not in a good way.

The rest of the week passed fairly uneventfully; I spent most of it trying to phone people whom I thought might be potential buyers for the Smiths' Royal Worcester painted fruit vases, placing adverts for the sale, and wondering where Albert and I would be going on our mystery trip.

I picked her up about 11.30 a.m. on Saturday morning and was instructed to drive toward the Malvern Hills, which I duly did. I had rolled the canvas roof back and as the sun shone into the car, it was one of those good-to-be-alive days. As we passed through Malvern, I made a gentle enquiry as to where we were going, only to be told in no uncertain terms that Albert was in charge and she would give me directions; in fact, she had the very latest garage road atlas open on her lap.

'Left', 'Right', and 'Straight On' were her stock phrases and after about an hour or so, I began to notice a certain hesitancy creeping into her voice. That and the fact that some of the roads appeared very familiar, having driven down them fifteen minutes earlier, seemed to indicate that we both had no idea where we were going – but for differing reasons. On we drove, relentlessly, and by my reckoning we had now driven about 120 miles, but were only around 25 miles from where we had started.

I suggested that it might be an idea if she gave me a clue as to where we might be going, but Albert was resolute that she was in charge and would get us there – eventually.

'Once we've crossed this river, I'll know exactly where we are.'

I drove on, enjoying her company and the sun; in truth, I was fairly relaxed and the Citroën seemed to be behaving itself. Other than the fact I had no idea where we were going, all was well with the world. As time wore on, however, I started to think I might be some help in trying to locate the river that Albert thought was crucial to our destination. I had taught Geography, albeit very badly, but the exact location of the river was proving a stumbling block to me as well.

Round in circles we drove. There was a hint of desperation in Albert's voice. 'I just need to find this wretched river,' she said, staring down at the map on her lap.

I thought discretion was the better part of valour. I pulled over and explained to Albert that whilst I knew the area pretty well, I couldn't think of a river anywhere near where we were parked.

'It's this one here – look! The long, straight blue one on the map.'

I peered over and gently, very gently, pointed out that the long blue and very straight river on the map was in fact the M50, which we had crossed in both directions a number of times. In fairness to Albert, she took it well as we made our way to our final destination, which I discovered was Eastnor Castle. The castle is hugely atmospheric, looking very much how a castle should. Its biggest selling point for me was that not only did it have fabulous contents, but it was still very much a family home. When we walked around, it was clear that Albert shared my love of the contents as we passed a Puginesque table that had a wonderful Chinese vase on it. All in all it was a good trip and we made our way back along the 'river', having decided to call in for a drink at the Greyhound.

We pulled into the car park and saw that Jim was already in the pub. Inside he was holding court, standing at the oche to the dartboard; pint in one hand and dart in the other. Why he didn't turn professional was beyond me.

'Double five and I'm in here – Phil, I'm unbeatable tonight,' he said, as the dart bounced off the tyre around the board and rebounded into the lap of one of the farmer's wives sitting quietly at a table. This was followed up with, 'Bugger! Albert, he hasn't taken you out in that bloody death-trap car, has he?'

Who needs friends, I thought to myself.

Cash wasn't exactly flush, so I had perfected the art of slow drinking; Albert obviously understood the form as she ordered a tonic water.

'Lord knows why you're going out with him when I'm available,' was Jim's opening gambit, as the three of us sat down around one of those copper-topped pub tables; Albert just smiled. There was a mate covering your back and then there was Jim. He followed this up with, 'I reckon I ought to have a go at one of those dart tournaments – I'd be in with a chance.' I thought it politic not to mention Jim's last dart.

We sat there for an hour or so and talked about the week ahead. Jim had his livestock market, though thankfully I had managed to avoid the ones run by our firm; Albert had to prepare the marketing of a large country house that Lloyd and Gold were selling; and I had the 'Wurster vazes' to sell. It was time to leave and as Albert and I walked to the car, she linked her arm with mine – my only regret was that Jim wasn't there to see it.

It was the day of the auction and as I pulled into the sale-room I saw that there was a top-of-the-range Bentley parked up. We didn't normally have Bentley drivers come to our sales. The car had two main distinguishing features – firstly, it was bright, fire-engine red and secondly, the registration plate. I'm not sure what its letters and numbers were, but it looked as if they spelt SCRAP; which, of course, they couldn't have done.

I walked into the saleroom and Windy came striding – or 'parping' – towards me.

'Phil, him over there is all over them varses.'

Windy didn't do subtlety in any way at all and everyone in the saleroom could hear – and see – that he was referring to the man who was clearly the Bentley driver. His dress code was a cross between Private Walker, the cockney spiv from *Dads Army*, and Arthur Daley from *Minder*.

Shiny was a word that didn't do justice to his light blue suit, and he had on one of those enormous flat caps that 1930s racing drivers wore, but it was the shoes that caught the eye. I had seen patent shoes before, normally I associated them with dinner jackets and they looked very smart – but these were a light, sandy brown colour. If you can remember bars of Caramac, that was the colour of them. All of this and a bright red Bentley; the whole ensemble took your breath away. I wandered over towards him.

'Morning, sor. I like them vazes – 'ow much are they in fer?'

I told him I was hoping to get around £10,000 for them.

'I'll gi' yer five bags of sand now and save yer the trouble.'

I hadn't got a clue what he was talking about and my bewilderment must have been obvious to him.

'Bag of sand, sor – a grand – 'n I'll give yer five now to save yer the bother.'

It took time, but the penny dropped that he was trying to buy them before the auction for £5,000. I told him that there was bound to be other interest.

'Fair point, sor – does I 'av to register or 'owt?'

I took him to the saleroom office and got a form out to give him.

'Sor, you fill it in fer me.'

I knew that farmers in the cattle markets always used to give the clerks their cheque books for them to fill out; I assumed this was what he wanted. I asked him his name, 'John Smith, sor,' – this had a ring of familiarity to it – and then his address.

'Ar well, I'm a travelling man, sor. I'll be paying cash.'

This was in the years before money laundering laws and cash really was king. He pulled out a wodge of £10 notes from his jacket pocket that resembled an oversized Swiss roll. In those days, trust and cash spoke volumes in the auction world, but sadly they have long since gone; in today's world of rules and regulations, it is altogether a different business.

Cliff Atkins was the man who was taking the sale today; he used to drive into the saleroom car park, leave his car outside the front door and stride in minutes before the auction was due to start. Negotiating the Bentley would have definitely put him in a bad mood – it was a better car than his and it was parked in his space. Cliff's sports jacket had a neon-light red check running through it, which made sunglasses necessary and would be a match for the Caramac shoes.

His late arrival was all well and good, but ninety per cent of the time he had no idea what he was being asked to sell. He saw the whole sale solely as a business operation and to him the lot in question was almost a by-product. Cliff was very much the focused businessman. By contrast, I got too involved with the lots and also the vendors that I dealt with. I wanted to do well for my clients and my nerves sometimes turned me into a gibbering idiot – in fact, that is still the case today.

We were about twenty lots away from the vases and sure enough, there were the usual crowd of suspects that I expected to see competing for them, though I couldn't see 'our man' anywhere. My John Smith had fixed a reserve on the vases of £7,500 – put simply, this meant that if the bidding didn't reach that amount, then they wouldn't be sold. I was fairly confident that they would sell, but for them to make top dollar I needed the other John Smith to push the price up.

'Lot number 53, a good pair of Royal Worcester vases hand-painted with fruit – a pretty choice lot. Bid me.'

JCA read out what I had written on the sale sheets, with the exception of the 'pretty choice lot' bit, which was his contribution to the description. This was always the worst bit; it is a long-established saleroom custom that no one ever makes the opening bid. Eventually, someone put their hand up when Cliff asked for £5,000. Prior to working for a firm of auctioneers I had no idea how an auctioneer would ensure the reserve was met, but he is able to bid on behalf of the vendor until the reserve was reached. JCA was nothing if not a good auctioneer and a bystander in the room would never have known this was happening.

I still could not see the Bentley driver; the bidding was between a local collector and a lady who I knew farmed in Herefordshire, but I had not seen her bid on Worcester porcelain before. The price crept up to £8,800 and the hammer was about to come down when a fresh bidder shouted out from the back of the room. 'And nine hundred, sor!' It was the scrap man. He and the farming lady took the bidding up to £12,300, when she shook her head and the gavel came down.

'Name?' JCA asked.

'Smith, sor. John Smith.'

I walked over to the Herefordshire lady to thank her for her bidding. She explained that her family farmed apples and pears for a certain well-known Hereford cider and perry maker and, as the vases were painted with apples and pears, she thought they would be an ideal buy for her family – until John Smith No. 2 spoilt things.

Out of the corner of my eye, I could see him making his way into the office to pay; I thought I would pop over to make sure all was well. I walked in to where Hinge and Bracket were ensconced; they had smoked their way through a couple of packets of Benson and Hedges and the atmosphere resembled 'Purple Haze' by Jimi Hendrix. Mr Rayer sat in the corner of the office lighting his pipe, which added to the smog and meant you could have smoked a kipper in there.

I watched as John Smith paid for his purchase from the roll of tenners and I was going to get a box for him when Mr Rayer shouted over, 'I've got one of the men to pack them for you!' My heart sank at this, as most of 'the men' were Mr Rayer's hangers-on, who were better suited to hitting things with a big hammer than packing fine porcelain. I escorted the new John Smith out of the smoke-filled room; I'm not sure either of us could see where we were going.

'I 'spect yer wondering 'bout me name, sor?'

I had to admit it did seem somewhat coincidental that the seller and the buyer both had the same name. It transpired that they were from the same travelling family, and the one John Smith wanted to sell and the other John Smith wanted to buy. They had decided that putting the vases into auction was the best way to get a fair price for both John Smiths. I was delighted that all had ended so well.

A few days later, I walked into the office to see Hinge and Bracket looking at me in a slightly confused manner, each waiting to give me a message. Hinge said, 'A Mr John Smith phoned and said thank you for helping with the vases,' and then Bracket said, 'A Mr John Smith phoned and said thank you for helping with the vases.'

Sometimes it's easier not to explain things – and who said you can't act for buyer and seller?

Chapter 3

The Cat House

Life didn't seem too bad. Albert and I were going along quite nicely, I was gathering a bit more confidence and success at work, and whilst it wasn't exactly a Ferrari, the Citroën did seem moderately reliable.

Despite Mr Rayer's desperate attempts to take me down the agricultural path in my career, I was beginning to enjoy the saleroom side of the business. I had seen my father scratch a living from the land; it was a lot of hard work and I felt that a business owing its fortunes to the weather was not for me.

I was never quite sure whether my father was proud of me, because I was making my way in what he regarded as a profession, or whether he was disappointed in me, because I had no intention of becoming a son of the sod. Farming and agriculture are definitely a way of life; long hours in all weathers for, in our case, little or no reward. There is no doubt that some people have made a lot of money out of the land, but none of them were called Serrell.

My father seemed to accept that this was his lot in life and on more than one occasion when I talked of a holiday abroad, or some such fanciful notion, I was brought quickly down to earth with, 'Our sort don't do that, son.' He not only accepted his lot, but appeared to have little or no ambition to change things. That was not for me.

I walked into the office one Monday and Hinge, lighting her third cigarette for the morning, told me that we had just had a phone call from a lady who wanted us to clear her mother's house on the west side of the river in the city. That was meat and drink to a general practice firm of auctioneers and as I drove out to the property, I was imagining all the most wonderful things I might find there – good Victorian furniture, silver and probably some local Worcester porcelain – it was a journey into the unknown.

I pulled up outside the property. It was in the middle of a three-storey terrace of Georgian houses that, due to demolitions and redevelopment, now found themselves in the middle of a bunch of nondescript 1960s bungalows. I walked up the long path to the front door and was greeted by the daughter. She was probably about fifty years old and told me that her mother had died three months earlier; the local firm of lawyers who were dealing with the estate had recommended not only our firm, but me in particular to deal with the estate.

'My mother had a strange obsession,' the daughter said, as we walked into the hall. That was the biggest understatement since Noah remarked it looked like it was going to rain.

Cats.

They were everywhere. There were cats made out of china, glass, tin and wood, paintings of cats, prints and cats in pretty much every medium you could imagine. I looked around the whole house and this was definitely a quantity not quality job. I explained to the lady that there was nothing here of huge value; only a few lots that would be sold separately, but the majority in big quantities or boxfuls.

'It doesn't matter,' she said, 'it was Mum's wish for her cats to go to auction and I want to see her wishes through. I won't be checking up, but I feel duty bound to come to the auction and see them sold.' She added, 'The thing is, we need to sell the house quickly and the estate agent wants the house cleared before we put it on the market.'

This was a job for Big Nige, our trusty haulier. Nigel used to wander around the saleroom with a grand piano under each arm and, more importantly, he was gun-barrel straight. Being able to trust a haulier was possibly the greatest qualification for the job. He would clear a house like this in his sleep and I reassured the lady client that there would be no problem. I drove back to the saleroom and called Nigel straight away.

'Would love to help you, Phil, but we're off to Weston on our holidays for two weeks.' Weston-super-Mare had been the destination of choice for Big Nige's family for many a year. This was not what I wanted to hear – it was time for plan B; except I didn't have one.

I gave Albert a lift home and on the way we called in at the Greyhound. Jim's car was already parked outside; it could have been Jim's office, he spent so much time there. The three of us sat down, staring at two halves of bitter and a tonic water, wondering how to overcome my cat-clearing problem. Jim suggested trawling through the *Yellow Pages*; I politely let him know that I had spent most of the afternoon doing exactly that without any success at all.

'We could always hire a van and do it ourselves at the weekend,' ventured Albert.

'Bloody hell, Albert. You must like him!' was Jim's response – and thinking about it, he must have been right.

I pointed out to Albert that there was so much stuff in the house that it would take us about five weekends to clear and I simply didn't have enough time for that.

It was at this point that a stranger walked into the bar. The Greyhound was a bit spit-and-sawdust and a proper old-fashioned village pub. It's à la carte menu was a choice of pork pies, pickled eggs and a variety of crisps. There was a big fireplace with a roaring fire that had half a tree on it, and old horse brasses scattered randomly on the wall with an out-of-date *Farmer and Stockbreeder* calendar showing the different breeds of sheep you could have.

It was a bit like an extension to the cattle market in that the standard dress for the men folk was a sandy coloured smock with baler twine around the waist, and a pint of Bathams Best Delph Bitter in front of them. Most of the ladies wore their Sunday best whatever day of the week it was and drank either stout or snowballs – with, of course, the obligatory cherry on a stick.

The general hubbub of chatter stopped when any stranger walked into the bar. The scene was similar to one of those grainy 1960s black-and-white films where the hero walks in to a local pub and everyone stops talking, turns around and stares at him. (In the films, he's normally discovered the next morning with an axe between his shoulder blades and the whole village keeps quiet. I'm pleased to report that this didn't happen at the Greyhound.)

We carried on our conversation as the stranger came and sat at the table next to us and frankly we were drawing a blank. After a time, the stranger got up to leave and turned to our table saying, 'Look, I hope you don't mind, but I've just over-heard what you've been talking about and I've got a van and a few men that work for me; I'm sure I could have the place cleared in no time at all.' As he walked out, he gave me a piece of paper with his name – Sid Carter – (you will appreciate I have changed his name) and a telephone number on it. It was manna from heaven for me, though my two companions didn't share my view.

'Phil, I'm really not sure you should instruct a complete stranger,' was Albert's view, whilst Jim's was a little more forthright.

'Mate, I'd give him a wide berth – he's got suede shoes on.'

I couldn't quite see the relevance of the shoe remark, but it was a salient point in Jim's mind. As far as I could see, I was between a rock and a hard place, as I didn't have any other options and time was against me.

I got to the office next morning and called Sid.

'How big's the house?' seemed a fair opening question. I told him that it was a Georgian townhouse with a long front garden, so whilst it was a fifty-yard walk to the road, it was all flat.

'And what d'you reckon it's going to cost the lady?'

I had absolutely no idea, but told him I thought somewhere between £500 and £1,000.

'Mate, I'll do it for five hundred.'

Well, that seemed more than fair and I arranged to meet him at the house that afternoon, after I telephoned the lady client to fix the appointment. Later on, I got to thinking I wasn't sure how Sid could quote for a job he hadn't seen, but I suppose he knew his business. I also told him that we would pay him once it was finished and all the cats and everything else in the house had been sold.

We met at the house and I showed Sid around.

'No worries, mate – leave it to me.'

I explained to my client that I couldn't produce a full receipt for her of the lots we were taking, as it would simply not be cost effective; not only that, but it would take too long as there was so much in the house. I also said that we wouldn't put all the cats in one auction, but feed them into a number of sales. There's only so many cats people want and I didn't want to flood the cat market; in fact, it could take three or four sales to sell them all.

'We'll make a start now,' said Sid. 'The lads are in the van.'

Sid was my knight in shining armour. It was a load off my mind and, as a matter of courtesy, I called the lawyers to thank them for the recommendation and tell them what I proposed to do .

All seemed to go well over the coming days, as load after load of cats made their way into the saleroom, with Windy being given the task of herding them up into lots. Everywhere you looked, there was a cat staring back at you. 'And that ain't the half of it, Phil, there's boxes of the things out the back. I reckon it'll take about four sales to get rid of this lot!'

As the sales came and went, the demand for cats was buoyant and my client was there to witness every one of them find a new home. I was running the auction equivalent of the Cats Protection League. It had all gone well and Sid had proved to be a bit of a star – something I was not slow to point out to Albert and Jim.

'Phil, you mark my words,' Jim warned me. 'Never trust a man with suede shoes.' He never expanded on where this theory came from.

About two weeks after the last cat sale, my lady client telephoned the office.

'Philip, have you sold everything from my mother's house now. Has everything gone?'

Thankfully, yes. Every last one of them had now left the saleroom.

'Did you sell everything through the saleroom or did you sell any privately?'

I wasn't sure where this was going, but everything always went through the auctions and nothing was sold by private treaty.

'The thing is, Philip, I was driving home last night and went past an antique shop and there were two cats in the window. They were about two feet tall and bright blue with red spots on them. I'd forgotten about them, but when I saw them in the shop, I knew they hadn't been through the auction.'

This was worrying and I called Sid up straight away. My thought was that he had left the back of his truck open whilst ferrying stuff from the front door to his van and someone might have stolen a box out of the back. Sid was adamant this couldn't have happened.

'What's this all about. Has something gone missing?'

I told him about the big blue cats in an antique shop and that I would have to discuss the matter with my client to see what she wanted to do.

'I haven't had them – me and the lads would never nick anything.'

That was a strange thing to say. I hadn't made any such accusation, but the whole situation made me feel very uneasy. The next morning my client called me on the phone.

'Philip, this is very strange, but I drove past the antique shop again on my way home and the cats weren't in the window anymore. I called into the shop and she said a young lad had been in and bought them.'

I was not sure what a rat smelt like, but I could smell one – this all seemed far too coincidental. I rang up Sid again, who sounded very uncomfortable on the phone. Not for one minute did I think that the antique shop had done anything wrong, I would imagine they were as innocent as I was, but there was a slow dawning on me that Sid had not been quite as honest and upright as he might have been. I decided to tell Sid that I had no intention of paying him the £500 haulage bill that was outstanding and that if he wanted to pursue it, he would have to instruct lawyers.

I rang up my client and told her what I had done; financially she was happy, as in her view the cats were not worth a great deal, but the whole episode left a very nasty taste in my mouth.

There was still one matter that I had to deal with. I had been recommended to the lady by a local firm of lawyers, who were dealing with her mother's estate, and was now in a quandary as to whether I should tell them what had happened. If they didn't know, I would alert them to the fact that we had used a potentially untrustworthy haulier, but if I didn't tell them and they knew, they might view my actions less than favourably. I decided to call and tell them exactly what had happened.

'Don't worry, Philip, we all get a wrong 'un now and then. Thanks for telling us.'

I never heard from or saw Sid again.

The next few weeks passed relatively smoothly, with sales coming and going, and nothing too spectacular to report. Mr Rayer was still very keen for me to follow in his agricultural footsteps, which presented me with something of a dilemma. I had no intention of becoming an agricultural surveyor, as my heart simply wasn't in it, but at the same time I felt that I was letting him down. He had been so good to me since I had turned my back on teaching and entered the auction world. I had developed the skill of creeping past his office, avoiding the bellow 'Philip!', and had succeeded till one fateful Thursday evening.

'Tomorrow I've got to pop out to do a live and deadstock valuation at Old Doings and could do with your help.'

Basically this meant going around a farm and counting stuff that stood on the ground – animal or vegetable – and arriving at a valuation. I was never quite sure why, but I always imagined it was for some tax reason.

'I'll meet you at the office at nine o'clock.'

I was doomed; still, I felt I owed it to him, so it was a small price to pay. It was going home time and I'd got into the routine of picking Albert up in the morning and taking her home at night. As we made our way back to Keane House, Albert dropped a bomb on me.

'My parents would love you to pop over for drinks and dinner tomorrow evening.'

It was a very kind offer and, even more importantly, a sign that I was being accepted by her parents. Nervous didn't even get close to describing how I felt. Albert's parents moved in different circles to the Serrell family – the only ones my folks moved in were crop circles.

This opened up all sorts of nightmares for me; not the least of which was spending a night trying to make small talk with her father. Quite simply, I thought we had nothing in common other than a mutual interest in his daughter and cars. And if I'm being completely honest, my interest in his daughter was probably not the same as his, and his interest in cars was likely to be more mechanical than mine.

My other major worry was that Albert might receive an invite to my parents' house for dinner and have my mother dish up *Spam Spaghetti à la Serrell* followed by Battenburg Surprise – the surprise being that it was inedible.

'We normally have a drink at 6.30 and then eat in the dining room.'

I don't recollect my parents ever had anyone round; they were very much of the TV supper types, and watching the telly sometimes took your mind off what you were eating.

I was in the office bright and early, ready for my trip out with Mr Rayer. I had no idea where we were going and there was little point in asking, since all I would get was, 'Out to see Old Doings.' We drove towards the Shropshire and Worcestershire borders and I sat back and relaxed as much as you could with Mr Rayer's driving. In between pipe-lighting, it was relatively incident free – we managed to stay on the road and didn't hit any cows that had wandered out of a field.

As we passed through one of those unspoilt villages with shops selling the barest essentials, Mr Rayer pointed to the pub and said, 'The farm's only just up the road – we'll pop back there for a bit of lunch.' This was all very well, but I had stressed to Mr Rayer that I needed to be back home for six o'clock at the latest. He promised we would be back, but I had past experience of events overtaking the day, and time going out of the window. Mr Rayer was not a man governed by the clock.

The morning passed with little to report other than to confirm that wandering around farms, ankle deep in cow manure and looking at various root vegetables, held little interest for me. I was sent by my boss to a far-off field to count sheep. I have never understood why this process was intended to send you to sleep, because it got me more and more agitated. It wouldn't be so bad if the wretched things stood still, but they kept wandering around.

I could see there were about 60 or 70 sheep in the field, but I couldn't get my count anywhere near that. I either got to

143 and gave up, because I had counted so many of the things twice, or I was concentrating so hard that when I got to 35, I wasn't sure whether I'd really got to 34, or was it 36? In the end, I'm ashamed to say I gave up. I decided to guess and strode back to my boss to tell him with an air of conviction that there were 67 sheep in the field. I still feel guilty about it to this day.

'Good, Philip, it's time for a bit of lunch. We'll wander back to that pub in the village.'

I gently reminded him that I had to be back by six, which got the response, 'Don't worry I haven't forgotten. We've just got a bit of machinery and a silage clamp to look at this afternoon.' I could hardly contain myself with excitement.

We drove back to the village, which was a quiet sort of a place, and pulled into the pub car park. The old Triumph coughed and popped, doing a very passable impersonation of Windy as we drove up the drive and parked outside the front door. We walked in and Mr Rayer ordered two pints of the local bitter and two pork pies.

I had gone straight over to a table in the window overlooking the car park and waited whilst Mr Rayer brought lunch over. I knew there was no point in offering to help him – he was a man who didn't do help – though this didn't stop me feeling guilty as others in the pub watched 'this poor disabled man' struggle on his own. He had a unique walking style: he kicked out his tin leg so that it landed a pace in front of him, and the rest of his body followed suit. It would have been impossible for most folk to carry our lunch the way he did, but Mister Rayer was a different gravy to most folk.

We sat down and watched the world go by as we savoured our lunch; I used to love these times listening to him and how the business used to be. The firm was originally founded in

1791 and had a great history. Mr Rayer was telling me about a sale it had conducted for Lord Coventry, whose country home was Croome Court, designed by Lancelot Capability Brown, with some of the rooms designed by Robert Adam – Brown was also responsible for the gardens.

It was a five-day sale just after the Second World War, when they sold about 150 lots a day; he described some of the lots that were offered, which would be worth a king's ransom now. Today most auctioneers would tackle that lot in one day, but life was very much different then.

Halfway through this story, which would normally have me captivated, it was obvious that he had lost my attention.

'You're not your usual self today, Philip,' he commented.

I could only reply, 'Look!'

The Triumph was rolling down the drive backwards towards the road. It was slowly gathering momentum as it crossed the road and hit a tree, boot first, on the far side.

'I thought that handbrake was a bit slacker than it should be,' he observed calmly. 'These pies are awfully good aren't they, Philip, and the hops really come through in this bitter.'

The fact that his car had taken off on its own, with the possibility of causing a horrible accident if anything had been coming along the road, didn't faze him at all. That was Mr Rayer all over – I suppose if you'd had people trying to shoot you during the war, a car rolling down a hill was not too much of a problem.

'We'll ask the landlord if we can phone up Old Doings and get him to come and tow us out.' Which is what we did.

By the time we made it back to the farm it was about 3.30 p.m., we had about an hour's work to do and another hour's drive back to the office. It was going to be tight. After arriving at the farm, I managed to tie the bumper back to the boot with the judicious use of a bit of wire, and then we carried on looking at tractors and the silage clamp; for the uninitiated, a silage clamp was – at least to my uneducated eye – a pile of rotting grass that was used to feed cattle.

Bless Mr Rayer, he was determined that I should be back in time and we were heading home by 4.45 p.m. When he was in a rush, you didn't want to be on the road if he was coming the other way; he had the driving technique of a pilot steering a toboggan down the Cresta Run – single-minded didn't come close to it. We made the Worcester office bang on six o'clock, with the bumper falling off for the fourth time as we pulled into the car park.

I hadn't got time to call in at home to freshen up, so I hurtled the Citroën round to Keane House, pulling into the drive at about 6.26 p.m. I knocked on the front door and Albert appeared almost immediately.

'Gosh, you're a bit late. Dinner will be ready shortly. Let's have a drink.'

I walked in to the drawing room and Albert's mother looked sort of pleased to see me. I wasn't sure what her father thought, as his newspaper remained firmly in front of his face.

'Well, Philip, tell us about your day. What have you been up to?'

So I regaled Albert and Mrs Albert about counting sheep and Mr Rayer's car rolling into the tree. I decided the best course of action was to ignore Mr Albert, as he seemed to be ignoring me.

'Mr Rayer sounds such a lovely character, doesn't he, dear?' said Mrs Albert, turning to her husband. The three of us turned to look at Mr Albert. It seemed like an eternity, but eventually the paper lowered, and he smiled at his wife and said, 'Yes, dear . . . charming.'

I'm not sure anyone had ever referred to Mr Rayer as charming.

'Well, let's go and eat. Rosemary said how much you like moussaka, so I've made that.'

Thank the Lord for that – I was looking forward to dinner and anything was better than Spam. I had eaten moussaka only once before, but really enjoyed it and as Albert had said her mother was a good cook, this was going to be a real treat. We sat down and Mr Albert looked at me and enquired, 'Wine?' I wasn't sure if it was a question or an instruction, but guessed the former and answered, yes please. He poured me a glass of what proved to be a lovely Chianti.

Wine in the Serrell household was a rarity. Nothing really went with Spam, but on high days and holidays my father would crack open a bottle of Blue Nun. The thing was, he would drink it out of a half-pint glass topped up with lemonade, rather like a Blue Nun shandy. I could never understand why it hadn't taken off in the trendy wine bars. After what would be a lovely dinner tonight, I was even more anxious that my parents might return the invite to Albert; I wouldn't wish the full range of Serrell hospitality on my worst nightmare.

Anyway, I was looking forward to my meal and the taste buds were galvanised into action with the appearance of garlic bread. Then Mrs Albert appeared with the moussaka. I must admit it didn't look too much like the one I'd had before; the layers of pasta weren't obvious, nor was the cheesy sauce that covered the mincemeat. I assumed that Mrs Albert was working from her own recipe and I had no doubt it would be lovely.

As the guest I was served first and my heart sank as spoonfuls of aubergine were ladled onto my plate. I'm sure aubergine is a wholesome and pleasing vegetable, but not to me; I didn't like the texture on my teeth and the taste was pretty horrid, too. This was nothing like what I was expecting. I had no option other than to trawl my way through it, but as soon as I had finished off my plateful, Mrs Albert put another very large spoonful in front of me with the words, 'Rosemary told me you had a healthy appetite!'

Through the course of the meal I discovered that it wasn't only me that Mr Albert didn't speak to; he didn't say much to anyone. This was probably because Albert and Mrs Albert did nothing but chatter all the time – they were obviously very close. Eventually I finished off my plate and with a huge sigh announced what a fantastic moussaka it had been and how full I was, before Mrs Albert could pile on any more.

I decided it was time to earn a few brownie points and offered to wash up with Albert's assistance. After her parents had retreated into the drawing room, we started to clear the table and Albert whispered, 'You didn't like that, did you?'

I couldn't lie and told her that I hadn't particularly enjoyed it. The one I'd had before was full of layers of pasta and cheesy sauce with mincemeat. Albert immediately saw the problem. I had meant lasagne, but said moussaka.

I never had this problem with Spam.

Chapter 4

The Sound of Breaking Glass

I was enjoying life in the saleroom and things didn't seem to be going badly. Getting up in the morning and looking forward to going to work every day was a good position to be in; I began to realise how lucky I was to have a job that I liked so much. It also reaffirmed my decision not to pursue a career in teaching.

I had spent three very happy years at Loughborough College of Physical Education, where they did their very best trying to turn me into a teacher of PE and Geography. I'm afraid the raw materials they had to work with weren't up to much – nonetheless I did leave there with a piece of paper telling me, and the world, that I was a teacher.

It was a job I wasn't cut out to do, but I thoroughly enjoyed my time as a student there. It was three years of playing rugby and cricket, as well as doing in-depth research into the local public houses and breweries. I still keep in touch with some of my old college mates, and there is no doubt that teaching is a vocation and there are some very good teachers about. However, I was never going to be one of them.

The people I met in the auctioneering world were so diverse, as were the items we dealt with, and that was what made the job so special. The saleroom was also full of rich characters and that included the punters as well as the staff.

There was a sort of dealers' dress code. Those who bought and sold period oak furniture wore yellow or pink corduroy trousers with brown brogues; silver and jewellery dealers were always immaculately turned out; while general furniture dealers were more jeans and jumpers. There were exceptions to the rule, but it was amazing how often it was proved right. Occasionally we would play a game by guessing what a newcomer into the saleroom would buy; very often we were right.

One saleroom regular was Timothy Galton and his dress code didn't give too many clues as to what he might buy, but he was clearly from what my mother used to refer to as good stock. He wore a dark blue, double-breasted blazer, white shirt with bow tie, a deep red or burgundy cashmere V-neck sweater, yellow corduroy trousers and the aforementioned brown brogue shoes. This sounds an acceptable ensemble, but it was all rather tired; in fact, very tired.

Timothy was also a very messy eater, which didn't help his appearance. Red and brown sauce stains with liberal dashes of gravy were the base colours of his shirt and jumper, but you could expect the occasional splattering of scrambled egg or sherry trifle to add a bit of colour. On balance, his appearance perhaps did reflect his taste in stock – both had seen better days.

Timothy was an interesting man, who was well-educated. During a conversation we had some time back, we were talking about schools and I asked him where he went. 'Slough Grammar' was the reply. It wasn't a school I'd heard of – until Mr Rayer told me gently it was another way of referring to Eton College by those in the know.

Timothy – never Tim or Timmy – had a very good eye for objects; there had been money at some time in the Galton family, but it was in the past tense. Silver, jewellery and small items that would today be known rather pretentiously as 'objects of vertu' were his chosen areas of expertise. The only problem was that Timothy's finances appeared to have fallen from grace since his schooldays, and he was definitely a champagne buyer on a beer budget.

Timothy would not compromise on taste, however, so the items he bid on were always damaged or had some problem with them. He never bought a good lot in perfect condition, as his budget of £200 meant he simply couldn't afford it. Occasionally he would leave commission bids (if you can't attend a sale in person, you can leave a commission bid with the auctioneers who will bid on your behalf), and I would drop off the lots he had bought at his home.

This wasn't something I normally did, but his car was a mirror image of himself, with rust patches around the wheel arches the colour of his brown-sauce stained jumper. It was a big old 1970s Vauxhall saloon, with a velour interior that looked like someone had eaten a meal off the seats – and left half of it behind.

Timothy lived in the coach house of a large country house on the outskirts of Hereford, which was completely at one with his clothes and his car; it was tired and frayed around the edges and in need of a good clean. His purchases littered – a more than apt word – his home. There were cracked Sèvres cups, bent silver candlesticks that had been dropped on the floor, beautiful snuff boxes with broken hinges; it was a museum of what not to buy. Like Timothy, nothing was perfect.

There's an old expression in the antique trade that I would commend to everyone: 'If the only thing you have to apologise for is the price, you're on the right tracks.' Unfortunately no one had ever mentioned this to Timothy, or if they did, he hadn't heard it. As an antique dealer, his restricted budget led to inevitable problems, because he would only buy damaged goods that were then difficult to sell. He was, for all that, a lovely and interesting man.

The saleroom could sometimes be a machine with a huge conveyor belt of goods passing through it, and the never-ending variety of lots reflected the owners and houses that they came from. We were currently clearing a Victorian house in Malvern, one of the many stone houses that are perched on the side of the hills. It was the usual fare of Victorian furniture, china and glassware. I saw the role of the auction-eer as a distribution centre or more accurately a redistribu-tion centre. As families moved out of the area and these Victorian stone piles were sold, we were charged with selling the contents that, more often than not, were normally bought by the homes' new owners.

There was nothing too exceptional in the next sale, though my eye was caught by a good pair of Regency glass lustres. Lustres are glass candlesticks with triangular glass droppers or prisms hanging from them. Their purpose was to reflect light throughout a room and originally they would have sat on a sideboard or table. These were completely clear glass; when the Victorians started making them, they often did so using coloured glass. They painted them with bright flowers and added chintzy bits of gilt; it was an era when less was definitely not more.

These were the real McCoy; I could see a good period oak buyer – complete with yellow cords – buying them to deco-rate a good eighteenth-century oak table. Lustres such as these were invariably damaged or had a dropper missing, but these were in mint condition; almost as if they had never been used.

On sale day they created a fair amount of interest and my guess was right, in that as well as a specialist glass dealer, a couple of good period furniture buyers were having a serious look. I thought they should make £200–300 and the level of interest seemed to indicate that I might be right. The lots before the lustres were all from the same house but nothing like the quality.

Meanwhile Timothy was buying his usual stock: a tortoise-shell tea caddy with half the tortoiseshell missing; a lovely Derby vase and cover, except the finial had broken off the cover; and a small silhouette that was torn in the corner. Things didn't change. I had often chatted to him about what he bought and he told me that he didn't want to compromise on taste or quality. Timothy didn't seem to appreciate that a good thing ceased to be a good thing when it was wrecked.

I made my way over to the far side of the saleroom. I wanted to see what the lustres made and had a passing interest in who bought them. Today was the same as every other day; the saleroom was packed with a complete cross-section of auction room society.

There were the ladies who never bought or sold a thing, but were in the same seat at every sale with their knitting, tinfoil-wrapped sandwiches and a flask of coffee, religiously recording the price every lot made. For some people it was a social club and they occasionally bought the odd lot, though there was no pattern at all to their spending; there were the part-timers who bought and sold things on the quiet to augment their income or pension; then there were the full-time dealers who were there to make a living – it was a day's business.

My wandering mind was snapped back to reality as I heard the lustres were about to be offered. The glass dealer opened the bidding at £200 and he and a furniture buyer specialising in dining-room pieces took the bidding up to £560, when the furniture dealer dropped out.

'£560 for the third and last time then ... look out, fresh bidding ... £580 – £600 – £620 ...,' and at that the hammer fell.

I was delighted as it was a really good price, which was confirmed when the glass dealer walked past me and said, 'Hell of a price for those lustres, Philip – I went £100 more than I wanted to.' It was a common occurrence for a dealer to tell me he had bid more than he wanted to and it emphasised the point that there wasn't a finite price on any object; it was all very subjective.

I walked outside to see Timothy loading his car with the day's haul; the boot was open and he was piling stuff into it. It was not dissimilar to a skip full of broken bits and bobs. I asked him if he'd had a good day

'Really pleased, Philip – particularly with the glass. Cost the money, but I think I've got someone for them.'

I wasn't sure which lot of glass he was talking about, as I hadn't seen him bidding on any of the glass lots. Imagine my surprise when he came out with the lustres. I watched as he placed them gently on top of the mound of damaged detritus in the boot of the Vauxhall, and carefully made sure they wouldn't move about by placing packing paper around them. I was amazed, as I had never seen Timothy either spend so much or buy such a good lot. Perhaps at last he'd heard that old adage about only apologising for the price; I was really pleased for him. Mind you, the next time he had a stall at an antique fair, the lustres would put the rest of his stock to shame.

I watched as he slammed the boot lid of the car – it was one of those horror moments when I could see exactly what was going to happen, but couldn't do anything to stop it. The lustres were about two or three inches proud of the boot and as the lid came down, it sheared the sconces – the tops – off; the symmetry of the break was almost perfect.

There was nothing I could say. Timothy just stood there staring at the nearly shut car boot hovering over the shattered remains of the Regency lustres – he then looked up at me and I returned his wounded stare. Silence. We were unable to find any words that were suitable.

I walked back into the saleroom, glancing back at Timothy, who was still standing over a boot that was now full of broken stock. It's probably my imagination, but I could swear I saw a tear running down his cheek. He never did buy anything else as good as the lustres – I suppose it was difficult to devalue anything that was broken before you got it.

Salerooms are a theatre of drama with an ever-changing cast of actors and props, but the reality is that they are also places of work. To many dealers, the object in question is irrelevant; they are simply buying for a profit and the less it cost, the greater the profit. Windy and the other saleroom porters had the job of lining up all the furniture in rows and once that was done, the china and other 'smalls' were separated into boxes and any other container that would hold the 'useful' stuff that every household had; the more valuable lots were laid out on the table tops.

My job was to 'lot up' the sale, hopefully separating the good from the bad. This was the fairly tedious task of putting a sticky number on each lot and writing the description down on the sale sheets. The highlight of my cataloguing back then was to pile the contents of a sewing box into a battered Victorian mahogany commode, which I then wrote down on the sale sheets as: 'Lot 15 – Commode and contents'. It was quickly pointed out to me that this probably wasn't the best description to sell the lot.

These were the sheets that the auctioneer worked from, and they formed part of the formal contract between buyer and seller. Other key parts to this contract were the falling of the gavel, and the auctioneer recording the price and the buyer's name. The skill to lotting up a sale was to try and create lots that were saleable – anyone can sell the Crown Jewels; the trick was trying to make a collection of battered old saucepans sound attractive.

The contents of the next sale were not overly inspiring. We had cleared a house in Worcester where a gentleman had died and we were acting on behalf of the family. I had met the son and daughter at the property, and it was evident that there was what my mother used to refer to as 'a bit of an atmosphere' between them. It wasn't so much chilly, as downright freezing. Their father had seen himself as a dab hand at carpentry; unfortunately, his ability fell shy of his ambition.

His home-made furniture was typified by one remarkable table that would have only been level on the side of a Welsh hill. How you could get four legs to be so different in length was beyond me. Each piece was subject to the roughest abuse from the coarsest-grade sandpaper – probably attached to a Black and Decker circular sander – and finished off with a coat of varnish with the consistency of semolina. Luckily the family had decided that the furniture would be divided between them, which was a godsend, because it was close to being unsaleable – though in fairness, the chairs he had made would fit readily around his table on that Welsh hillside.

'The one piece we would like to put into auction is this corner cupboard – I'd like to buy it,' the son told me, pointing down to a cupboard. It was unusual amongst his father's pieces in that the door was square, it appeared to shut and the shelves were level. The daughter then coldly added, 'I'd like to buy it too.'

I wasn't sure if there was a bit of 'history' between the two of them, but it seemed to be a case of where there's a will, there's a relative. I always thought it was a pity when families couldn't reconcile their differences, particularly when it was over a £30 corner cupboard.

The corner cupboard was lotted up next to two chests of drawers that had been delivered to the saleroom and entered by two different vendors. The first, lot 80, was a bog-standard, mid-Victorian example made out of mahogany with an arrangement of two short drawers over three long drawers – it was worth about £200. The chest next to it, lot 81, was essentially the same, in that it was made out of mahogany and had the same arrangement of drawers, but this is where the similarity ended. This one pre-dated the other by about thirty years and was made out of the best quality timber, and the drawers were flanked by finely reeded columns; it was all together a different kettle of fish.

Knowing what I know today, I would probably have guessed that it was made by Gillows, who were a Lancaster firm that was set up by Robert Gillow in the eighteenth century. Their furniture was normally made out of top quality mahogany and was typified by reeded legs and columns. They were patronised by the great and the good and even referred to in a Gilbert and Sullivan opera. I thought this chest might make between £500 and £600.

The sale view day was as busy as ever, with dealers trawling through the boxes of china looking for the hidden gem that I had missed, making notes and marking their scraps of paper with the lots they were interested in. All dealers used their own price code, so that if anyone looked over their shoulder at their bit of paper, they wouldn't have the first idea what their top bid was.

I tried all sorts of codes for my own valuations, but was never bright enough to remember any of them, which meant that valuations took forever as I tried to work out my own code – it completely defeated the object. (After years of fooling everyone else and myself with unfathomable ones, I now have a code that I can not only work with, but also remember.)

I chatted to one of the furniture regulars about the sale generally. 'Bloody good chest that, Phil, lot 81. What do you reckon it'll make?'

I told him what I thought and looked at his face to get his reaction. And I got . . . nothing. There must be a school for antique dealers where they learn how to give nothing away; you wouldn't want to play cards with any of them. My unsubtle questions were usually met with, 'I expect there'll be a bit of interest', 'We'll all be wiser when the hammer falls', or 'I'll watch it and see where we end up' – none of which told me very much.

The 'home-made furniture' family were also at the viewing in their two warring factions. It was vaguely amusing, if not a little sad, to see them skirt around the saleroom avoiding one another; not even daring to risk a glance at the opposing party. The stupid thing was that I knew the lot they both wanted to bid on, they each knew the lot they wanted to bid on, and they also knew the lot each other wanted to bid on.

Their father's corner cupboard meant it was going to be an interesting sale tomorrow.

Cliff Atkins, as usual, landed his car outside the front door of the saleroom and walked in five minutes before the start of the sale. There was nothing to report in the first half hour or so, until we arrived at the home-made cupboard.

'Lot 79, this fine corner cupboard ... bid me £50 someone?'

Silence – but I was sure it didn't merit the word 'fine'. JCA followed his opening gambit with, '£40, £30 then ... bid me?'

It was now about what I thought it was worth, but was aware there was likely to be only two bidders. Eventually the sister put her hand up – quickly followed by her brother.

'£30 – £35 – £40 – £45 – £50 – £55 – £60.'

This was double what the cupboard was worth. The brother was staring directly ahead looking at the auctioneer, and the sister was giving her brother what I believe are termed 'death stares'.

'£65 – £70 – £75 – £80 – £85 – £90 – £95.'

I glanced across at the two protagonists, neither of whom showed any sign of slowing down. '£100 – £110 – £120 – £130 – £140 – £150.' This was beginning to get a bit silly. '£220 – £230 – £240 – £250.' Some of the furniture dealers started to worry in case they were missing something.

'What lot are we on, Phil?' and when I told them, 'What, that 'orrible little corner cupboard that looks like it's come out of my son's woodworking class?'

JCA went on, '£380 – £390 – £400 – £410.' Not a trace of emotion from brother or sister and I was hoping that one of them would stop, as this was now getting more than silly.

'£520 – £530 – £540 – £550.' You could have bought a really good Georgian mahogany, bow-fronted, inlaid corner cupboard for that.

'£630 – £640 – £650 – £660. Any more then ... any advance on £660? Done and sold at £660!'

The gavel came down and the victor was the brother; the sister did not know what a lucky escape she had. Looking like thunder, she stormed out of the saleroom leaving her brother standing there with a smug, satisfied look on his face; I suspect it would vanish when he realised how much he'd paid for it. Meanwhile Cliff Atkins leant over and whispered very loudly in my ear, 'You got that wrong. You need to look at these things a bit more carefully.'

It did occur to me that if he had got there a few minutes earlier, he could have had a look at it and seen what I saw.

There's always a hubbub in a saleroom after a lot has made a good price or considerably more than expected; I was keen to hear what the two chests of drawers made over the saleroom chatter. Over the noise, I could hear, 'Any more then? £210 for the chest of drawers. Now, lot 81, the next chest ... stand on?' (Put simply, this is when an auctioneer asks for a bid the same as the last lot he sold.) A forest of hands shot up at £210 and continued to rise until the hammer eventually came down at £830.

It was a price I was pleased with, as I hoped the vendor would be. It was difficult to see how two examples of the same piece of furniture could be so different until they were side by side, as they were now in the saleroom; then the quality of the more expensive one was very apparent.

After the sale there was the general melee of buyers collecting their lots and vendors clearing any lots that might not have been sold. There was always a search for the right lots, normally amongst the smalls, where people have moved things around. Big Nige was on the door in a security capacity to make sure nothing was sneaked out that shouldn't have been. No one tried to get past Big Nige.

All was going well and the saleroom was clearing, but the buyer of the Gillows chest of drawers had come back to the saleroom, which was a bit worrying. I could see it had been taken and I hoped there wasn't a problem. The poorer of the two chests of drawers – lot 80 – was standing there in glorious isolation.

'Phil, where's my chest?' were not the words I wanted to hear. I walked over to the door and asked Big Nige if he knew where the Gillows chest was.

'Not sure I know Mr Gillows, Phil. Is he the feller with the yellow van who comes from Cheltenham?'

Bless Big Nige, he wouldn't have known a Gillows chest from a treasure chest. I described the chest to him and told him it was lot 81. 'Oh, old Gubbins took that – cleared it pretty much straight after the sale.' I told Big Nige he must have taken the wrong one, but he was quite adamant. 'I checked the receipt, Phil. Lot 81, Chest of Drawers.'

This seemed a bit strange, so I told the dealer who had bought it and was standing next to me that we should go and check in the office. We wandered off to see Hinge and Bracket, making our way through the haze of cigarette smoke, and told them what our problem was. Hinge handed me over the sale sheets to see for myself.

'There you are, look. *Lot 80, Chest of Drawers, £210*, with the buyer's name, and *Lot 81, Chest of Drawers, £830*, with the buyer's name,' and the man standing next to me was the buyer of lot 81 with his name on the sale sheets. Now I was really confused, as everything was as it should be. Bracket then handed me the unpaid purchaser's invoice and I could immediately see the problem. She had copied the lot numbers from the sale sheets and got them the wrong way round. The expensive chest had become the cheaper one and vice versa.

'It's a good job I haven't paid for it yet!' reacted the dealer standing next to me; it was said half in jest, but he was half serious. This was in the days before computerisation and I would have backed Hinge and Bracket against anything IBM had to offer; this was the only time I can remember them making a mistake. Hopefully that wasn't too much of a problem – I knew the dealer who had got the cheapest Gillows chest in the world and it was simply a matter of asking Big Nige when he had taken it, so I could give the dealer a call and rectify the problem.

'He left the saleroom about an hour ago,' was the answer; he would have just got back to his shop. I decided to give him a call. The antiques trade were generally a decent bunch of people and as this was a genuine mistake; I was sure once I explained it to him, it would all be sorted. I made the call and rather than having the problem rectified, was taken aback by the reply, 'Sorry, Philip, I've sold it.' This was a bit tough to believe and I asked him if when he was clearing the lot, he didn't think he'd got the wrong one; he surely knew he'd bought the cheaper chest and not the £830 one.

'Philip, I didn't really look at the chest, just the lot number. Sorry, but it's your error and anyway its gone now. Bye.' And he put the phone down – that was the end of that. I apologised to the dealer, who had heard the whole conversation.

'I'm not surprised, Philip. No one likes him and there's no way he's sold that so soon. He's just got a cheap chest, hasn't he?'

It was really annoying, but there was not much I could do about it. I decided tactically it would be better to tell Mr Rayer what had happened rather than Cliff Atkins. His attitude was a reassuring, 'Well, no one has died, Philip, and accidents happen.'

The bottom line was that it was going to cost money, as we were currently left holding a very average Victorian chest of drawers that stood us in at £830. All auction goers will know that nothing sells as well second time around the block as it does first time and this was no exception – it made only £170.

About two weeks later, a car belonging to one of the saleroom regulars pulled up. The driver was a retired bank manager who bought furniture from a variety of sources to restore and improve. Once he had given it the once over, his latest project was brought into the saleroom to be offered in one of our general sales. He wasn't bad, but that said, he wasn't good either. Many less charitable souls would have thought he'd be better off not bothering with the restoration bit, but his efforts augmented his bank pension.

'Here, Phil, come and have a look at this. I'd like to put it in your next sale.'

I walked out to his estate car and as he lifted the boot, I could see a blanket over a piece of furniture. As his latest project was revealed, I saw an almost exact copy of the home-made corner cupboard.

'I made it myself, Phil. I saw what that last one made in your sale and thought I could do as well as that.'

Well, he was nearly right.

Chapter 5

Partnership and Pigeons

Albert and I were with Jim in the Greyhound generally putting the world to rights and bemoaning the fact that we had no money. In the past, Jim and I had embarked on a venture into the market gardening world to grow produce to sell, but after the first flush of success it went horribly wrong – as well as being too much like hard work. There was no doubt something had to happen soon, as we had no money at all. Then Albert had a brainwave.

'Why don't we each chip in twenty or thirty pounds and buy and sell antiques. I wouldn't have thought we could lose much money – all the dealers seem to do quite well at it.'

Jim seized on this straight away. 'Bloody great idea, Albert; what we should do is buy a bit of furniture that we can restore. Buy cheap – sell dear; I like it. Phil, you'd better get on this.'

All this sounded simple, but I had a few reservations. Firstly, I wasn't sure that auctioneers should be dealers, as I thought it muddied the water a bit, and secondly, it did rely a lot on my judgement.

'That's agreed then. Phil, here's my thirty quid. If you're a gentleman, you'd better sponsor Albert.'

I wasn't sure if he was joking or not, but thankfully before I could say anything, she put £30 on top of Jim's stash and we were in business. All I had to do now was find something with a profit left in it.

I was in the Worcester office one morning, when Mr Rayer asked me if I would go and look at some old office furniture that belonged to a long-time client of his. I got the impression they had both served in the Second World War together. The family had one of Worcester's old businesses that had originally been set up in the mid-nineteenth century.

'Philip, they just haven't advanced with the times,' he said sorrowfully.

That was rich coming from a man who's idea of moving with the times was to use a 3B pencil and a small notebook rather than a Dictaphone. His notebooks themselves were worthy of a place in the Victoria and Albert Museum – Egyptian Sanskrit had nothing on these. They were about 4 inches by 3 inches and Mr Rayer had written on both sides and on every available space in every direction. All in a normally blunt 3B pencil; if he could have written on the edge of the paper, he would have done.

'Philip, if you get out one of the old valuation books, you'll be able to see what I put the stuff in at. It could have been a couple of years back, but it might help you.'

No, it most definitely wouldn't help. A few years back in the Rayer calendar could take us back to the Boer War and if I could find it – and it was a big if – I very much doubt I'd be able to read it.

'Make the appointment first thing, Philip – he likes to get on with his day.'

I thought that was a strange remark coming from a man with no concept of time, but I duly phoned the client in question and made my appointment to go and see him.

I made my way there for our 9.30 a.m. meeting. The address I had was on the outskirts of the city and was slap bang in the middle of rows of Victorian terraced houses. It was a factory unit built in the 1960s, when economy ruled over aesthetic. I'm not sure how they conspired to get it so wrong, but there was a lot of architecture in the 1960s that fell short of the mark and this factory unit was a prime example. Single storey, wire-cut facing brick under a corrugated asbestos sheet roof, the building was utilitarian at best and pig ugly at worst.

I walked in through a door that led into the main factory area, where there were about ten or twelve people working, but in its heyday there must have been fifty or sixty in there. It was so cold that I made my way quickly to the offices, which were at the far end of the factory. This was obviously a Mr Rayer job – the ladies in the office were all past pension age and were probably struggling with these new-fangled golf ball typewriters.

The office furniture was nearly as old as the ladies and had certainly seen some service. It was mainly rusting metal file cabinets and desks, mixed in with the odd bit of Government-surplus furniture. There was an overpowering smell of gas in the office, which came from the six old Calor gas heaters that had been strategically placed for optimum heat.

At the rear of the main office area was a row of partitioned-off offices with frosted glass panels, which at one time were designed to let the light in, but had long ceased to be functional. The big office was probably for the 'typing pool' and the smaller offices at the end were for the various managers who had once worked there. It looked as though these were no longer in use, as only one had a flicker of light shining through the glass.

One of the ladies directed me to the dimly lit office and knocked on the door.

'Come,' was the one-word response from within.

I walked in to the office equivalent of Miss Havisham's house in *Great Expectations*. There were files everywhere, most of which looked as if they hadn't been opened in years. My new client was seated behind a massive oak desk with another mountain of paperwork on it; scattered around the office were a number of old-fashioned tubular steel chairs with canvas seats.

'I expect Mr Rayer's told you,' he said, 'I'm closing down the business.' He hadn't, but there was nothing new there. 'I've sold the building and wondered if any of the office furniture was worth putting in one of your sales.'

Today those items would be regarded as trendy, vintage, and no self-respecting apartment would be without them, but this was then. The bulk of the stuff fell into the liability category, rather than asset.

The gentleman explained that not only had he and Mr Rayer been in the army together, they had also shared schooldays. He got up to show me around and we walked into the redundant offices, which were packed full of the same sort of stuff – stuff being the appropriate word! The whole place, including him, smelt musty.

In one room, with 'Wages Office' on the door, there was an Edwardian ebonised desk with a short bank of two drawers to each side, two drawers below the writing surface, and raised on turned legs. The problem was that it was ebonised or black.

Queen Victoria's devoted husband was Prince Albert and when he died in the 1860s – probably from exhaustion as he and Victoria had nine children – the whole country went into mourning with her. The Queen was distraught and it is said she mourned for the next forty years, which is the reason why she always wore black. In a way the country followed her and a great deal of ebonised or black furniture was produced. The desk was probably worth £100–150. If it had been made out of walnut, you could have added a nought on the end of that figure.

'What it's worth doesn't really matter too much – none of it stands me in at anything. I need it cleared as I have to give vacant possession with the building when I complete on the sale. Can you just come and pick it up and sell it for me?'

I spoke to Big Nige and we arranged a date to meet at the unit to collect the lots for sale; he was busy most mornings, so the earliest we could get there was about 11.30 a.m. Whilst I was mindful of Mr Rayer telling me to get there early, that didn't seem too late, so all was well. We arrived back at 11.30 on the appointed day, walked into the unit and made our way into the main reception office. One of the ladies, without saying a word, got up and escorted me to the head man's office and knocked on the door. The light was on, but there was no reply, so she knocked again.

'Yesh?'

I opened the door and walked in to see our client bending over by the bottom drawer of the filing cabinet. He got up very quickly and nearly fell over; sudden movement didn't seem a good thing. He sat down behind his desk and leaned back in his office chair, which was one of those 1930s oak swivel-type chairs that reclined. He went back a little too far, and nearly did a backward somersault into the waste paper bin. Big Nige and I helped him off the floor and it was soon apparent why he fell over backwards. He reeked of booze and was absolutely smashed. That would explain why Mr Rayer wanted me to get there early.

'I'll leave it to you – jush take everything to the shale.'

I told him to stay where he was in the chair and Big Nige and I went around making a list of everything that was to be sold. We would still be there now if we itemised every empty Bells whisky bottle we found. The drawers in all the desks and file cabinets were full of them. The only thing that was empty was the ebonised desk.

I left Big Nige to it and went back to the office to report to Mr Rayer. I told him all was in hand without going into too much detail; I had worked out that Mr Rayer and detail were probably best kept well apart. We chatted about his old friend and how he hadn't taken his business forward.

'Let that be a lesson to you, Philip. You need to move with the times.'

I looked around Mr Rayer's office at the mountain of files everywhere, copies of ten-year-old magazines, and maps on his desk with measurements in rods, poles and perches. It wasn't for me to say anything.

We had a board meeting of our new antique-dealing venture in the Greyhound that evening.

'Have you bought anything yet, Phil?'

Albert leapt to my defence. 'Give him a chance, Jim!'

The short sharp answer was no. I told them about my trip to the unit in Worcester, which Jim picked up on immediately when I mentioned the ebonised desk.

'Well, if you say it would sell better if it wasn't black, we'll buy it and strip it. Quids in!'

Jim was nothing if not an enthusiast.

The sale day for the ebonised desk arrived and Albert, Jim and I had agreed that we would go to a maximum bid of £90, which was the sum total of our capital. During the previous day's viewing, there had been little or no interest in the desk.

Anyone I spoke to about it came out with the same remark, 'Phil, it's ebonised – no one wants that. Be worth a grand if it wasn't.'

That seemed to reinforce the view that if we could buy it and strip it back to its natural timber, we might be able to make a profit. I still had a slight uneasy feeling about an auctioneer buying things in his own sale, but reconciled myself with the fact that we weren't going to try and flip it straight away for a profit. When it came up for auction, the bidding opened at £50 and went quickly to £80, where it came to a grinding halt. Shall I or shan't I, and before you knew it, I had – we were the proud owners of an Edwardian ebonised desk.

I went into the office and telephoned Albert and Jim, who by chance were both working in the Worcester office of Lloyd and Gold that day.

'That's great! We'll borrow your old man's Transit and pick it up later this afternoon.'

I sloped off and met Jim at my parents' house. My father never owned reliable vehicles and his Transit pickup truck was no exception; Jim and I had borrowed it before and reliability was not a key feature. It had the dodgiest gearbox in the world, which only my father seemed able to work out; the cogs in it moved around, so first gear could be in one position when you set off on your journey, then move to where third should be as you drove on. Driving it was an experience and it occurred to me that I was plagued by useless vehicles.

As Jim and I set off for the saleroom, my father shouted, 'Just watch the lights, they're playing up a bit!'

This was not good – 'playing up a bit' to my father was the equivalent to total malfunction in anyone else's world. It was light at the moment, but would be dark on the way home, so we had to wait and see what tricks were in store for us. We got to Malvern and loaded the desk onto the back of the pickup and set off on the return journey when it was getting dusk.

'Phil, I can see us making a real killing on this little beauty. It shouldn't be much of a job to get it back to natural wood.'

There spoke a man who spent most of his life in the livestock market up to his armpits in cows and sheep. All was well with the lights, so I wasn't sure what my father was talking about – until I went round a right-hand bend and the whole lot went out. We were plunged into darkness.

'Bloody hell, Phil!' was Jim's not overly helpful contribution. There was no traffic behind us, only a car coming the other way that flashed its lights and blew its horn. As we went past, the driver wound down the window and made a gesture that you wouldn't use in polite society, but it started out with one finger and progressed to two.

The strange thing was that the pickup only did the light thing around right-hand bends and at no other time.

'You've got to nurse her,' was my father's answer, when we parked up and put the desk into one of the barns. We had arranged to meet Albert so we could start working on the desk straight way. Jim went back to his car and came back with a huge tin of Nitromors paint and varnish remover, the coarsest grade of wire wool in the world and an orbital sander that would strip tar off the road.

'Come on then, let's get at it. Time is money.'

Jim poured half the contents of the Nitromors over the top of the desk, just as Albert walked in.

'Jim, are you sure you should be using that much?' she asked, as he pulled out a metal paint stripper and launched into the top with a vigour not usually associated with him.

The paint was coming off quite easily, so was half the timber underneath. I was a little worried that the wood was not all the same shade, but was doing a passable impression of Joseph's coat of many colours. I put that down to the cocktail of chemicals and water that Jim was covering the desk, Albert and me in. The fact that we knew his enthusiasm wouldn't last long was the only limiting factor to the amount of damage he could do.

Over the next few weeks, we managed to keep Jim out of the way whilst Albert and I stripped all the paint off and got it back to bare wood. It was time for a board meeting.

'Bloody hell, Phil! It don't look much like walnut to me.'

He was absolutely right – our wonderful Edwardian desk was made out of fish crates and fruit boxes. The more I thought about it, the more obvious it was that you wouldn't use expensive timber and then ebonise it; the point of using a classic timber was to see the grain. We had managed to spend £90 on a desk, about £10 on 'consumables', and ten man-hours to halve the value of our asset.

'What are we going to do with the bloody thing now?'

That was the burning question; I was really at a complete loss.

'I think we should put it back how it was and put it back in the sale,' was Albert's suggestion.

'And how the hell are we going to do that?' was Jim's contribution. My answer was to keep him well out of the way. I thought Albert's idea was a good one.

'We'll paint it black with some blackboard paint, then gently sand it down with some very fine sandpaper to take it back to the flat surface.'

So she and I spent the next week putting back what we had undone. It was a division of labour – I slopped the black paint on and Albert did the delicate stuff of trying to make sure it looked like it did before. Jim and I took it back to the saleroom in the Trusty Trannie, only in daylight this time.

'Wasn't that the desk you bought last time?' Windy was as perceptive as ever.

Come sale day, it wasn't so much whether we'd make a profit, but how much we might lose. I pestered every dealer who walked past it – and some who didn't – to see if they might buy it. The 'No's were pretty conclusive. I was beginning to panic. As it turned out, it did sell for a loss – it made £80. That was only because a dealer bought it who was feeling sorry for me; apparently Windy told him the whole sorry saga.

That was end of my dealing career.

Driving around the county when I was alone with my thoughts and the Citroën, I often wondered about the Wenlocks' bureau bookcase. It had been over eighteen months since I'd seen it, and I was still none the wiser as to whether I was right or wrong about its possible value. Perhaps it was the one that got away, but I hadn't seen it advertised in anyone else's saleroom.

Time had moved on, and Albert and I had formalised our relationship with first an engagement and then a wedding. Albert's mother seemed pleased with our marriage and even her father now acknowledged my presence, which was something of a relief. I was a little concerned, however, when he told me he wanted a quiet word with me – 'man to man', as he put it. I was living in hope that he wasn't going to tell me about the 'birds and bees'. It was a bit late for that.

'Philip, I just wanted to have a word about Rosemary and you.' My heart sank; he *was* going to tell me about the facts of life. 'It's just that her mother and I have been talking . . .'

I don't know who was more embarrassed – him or me.

'It's a little delicate and . . . I don't know really how to put it.'

I could now feel myself starting to go red.

'Well, we know that your nickname for her is harmless, but we would very much appreciate it if you could call her Rosemary, or Rose if you have to, but could you please not call her Albert anymore?'

Waves of relief swept over me like a condemned man hearing his sentence had been commuted. From that moment on, Albert was no more and I was married to Rose. My parents were delighted with the arrangement, as it finally got me off their hands, and my digestive system saw an end to the never-ending Spam and Smash diet.

The only minor fly in the ointment was that on our wedding day Jim thought it would be a real hoot if he locked me in a ball and chain and pretended to lose the key. This was great, except that he really did lose the key. My father came to the rescue after a quick journey home to collect a set of substantial bolt croppers, and a hacksaw to end all hacksaws. I could see Albert's – sorry Rosemary's – parents not quite seeing the funny side of things, whilst my mother thought it was all hugely amusing.

The real icing on the cake was that I was offered a partnership with the firm, which initially I was very excited about. J. Clifford Atkins went through the details of the partnership with me and, halfway through the negotiations, it dawned on me that I was going to have to borrow a five-figure sum from the bank to buy myself in. A partnership not only meant I was on the line to the bank for my loan, but also any monies or other liabilities the firm might owe in addition. In exchange, with the figures JCA worked out, I would be earning only a small amount more than I was currently earning.

Still, I felt that I was investing in my future, that it was a risk worth taking and hopefully things would work out. What it didn't change was me doing what I loved – going to houses never knowing what to expect, or what I was going to see.

My next job was a routine house call that didn't involve too much travelling, as it was less than a mile from the saleroom in Malvern. It was a fairly 'average' house surrounded by similar 'average' houses with no doubt 'average' contents. I knocked on the front door, and was greeted by a lady who asked me in and briefed me that she was dealing with the estate of a deceased relative, and the house contents had to be cleared.

I walked around the house and it was the usual fare of mainly low-end Victorian furniture and effects; there was nothing startling, but it was all saleroom fodder that would sell, but at a price. It was a complete house clearance and as any auctioneer will tell you, there will always be a hidden treasure or gem that creeps out of the woodwork to surprise you. Hopefully.

This was a difficult job and one of the hardest parts of it was to manage client expectations. As we walked into the sitting room, there was the statutory copper kettle and warming pan in the fireplace.

'What do you think these would make? I can remember polishing them as a child.'

It would be ungallant of me to discuss a lady's age, but if she polished these as a child, she was a lot younger than she looked; these were reproduction and had no age at all. She had a far greater degree of patina than either the kettle or the warming pan. I told her that sadly they wouldn't make a great deal of money at auction.

'Really?' she said, as we stood there staring at the offending metalware. Pregnant pause – or awkward silence – it amounted to the same thing as we stood there; it seemed a lifetime, but was probably only for a minute or so. 'Is that all?'

I have been asked this question so many times on so many different occasions and never understood why. I was aware that I was what my father called 'careful' when it came to valuations, but I always gave what I felt was a realistic opinion. We moved on to a pair of Staffordshire dogs; early nineteenth-century examples can be sought after and worth a lot of money. These were again reproduction and when I told her my auction estimate, it resulted in another 'Really?' followed by 'Is that all?' and an eternity staring at them.

This was the story of everything in the house. It was all saleable, but nothing was worth a decent amount of money and most would be destined for one of the general sales, rather than one of the catalogued antique auctions. Eventually, after we had looked at more of the same with similar results, I think she got bored of listening to me.

'It seems nothing's really worth what I thought and there's not much point in looking at more of the same. There's a few boxes of china in the spare bedroom, but I'll leave you to go through them in the saleroom.'

It was up to Big Nige to bring the contents into the saleroom, and for Windy to go through the myriad of boxes and their contents. Working in the auction world is often seen as a cool and trendy business to be in, and there's no doubt there is a glamorous side to it, especially when the big money lots are sold and make the headlines. However, trawling through boxes of reproduction copper warming pans and kettles is not high on the glamour list.

Rosemary's father was keen to help me in my new role as partner in the firm, particularly as I was the auction man. Bankrupt stock was most definitely not on anyone's glamour list, but he was adamant it would be a good thing for the firm to get involved in. So much so that he phoned me at the saleroom one day, saying, 'I've got a job for you.'

I was pleased, as it was further confirmation that I had been accepted by him, though I was concerned as to what type of job it might be.

'It's a warehouse that sells good quality household linen – about £40,000 worth.' This was not going to make headlines in the *Antiques Trade Gazette*. I tried to sound enthusiastic, but what the hell was I supposed to do with a warehouse full of towels. Too much work can sometimes be as big a problem as not enough; the saleroom was busy and I couldn't spare anyone to go and sort through the contents of a warehouse.

The Greyhound was still a watering hole for Jim and me, but Rose was back at our little house cooking an evening meal; thankfully Spam and Smash weren't on the dinner menu.

'Folks have made a lot of money out of those bankruptcy sales,' was Jim's answer to my predicament. That was fine but, somehow or other, every sale had to be prepared and lotted up. 'Ask your old man to help you. He'll sort it out and it'll be a great opportunity for him to get away from your mother.'

That wasn't a bad idea, and I decided to call in on the way back to my new home and ask my father if he could help. He had been scratching a living growing lettuces and other produce with the emphasis on scratching. When I walked in, my mother's immediate reaction was to ask if I'd come back for some 'good old-fashioned cooking'. I chose to ignore this and chatted to my father about the possibility of him helping with the linen sale.

'Well, it's been a bit quiet on the growing front,' was his way of saying he'd help me. In business terms, he could turn wine into water. He had been taking his produce to the markets to sell, but hadn't grasped the concept that you were supposed to sell stuff for more than it cost to grow it. He agreed to help and we arranged to meet at the warehouse in Worcester in a couple of days' time. I felt a little easier, as I now had some sort of a plan.

Back in the saleroom, the table tops were full of boxes of modern metalware and china that Windy had unpacked from the 'Really? Is that all?' lady. There was a wooden box at the end of one table that looked as if it had something in it.

'Bloody pigeons, Phil – two of 'em. Bloody pigeons.'

Sometimes Windy spoke in riddles. It must have been obvious I hadn't got a clue what he was talking about, as he took me on a wind-assisted walk over to the table where the box was.

As I took the lid off, I looked in; not believing what I was looking at. They weren't pigeons but doves, and not any old doves, but Royal Worcester doves. These were modelled by Ronald van Ruyckevelt, who with his wife Ruth worked at the local porcelain factory – not only that, but they were life-size and were made in 1972 to commemorate the Silver Wedding of Queen Elizabeth II and Prince Philip. As if that wasn't enough, there were only twenty-five of them made, with the first set given as a present to the Queen and Prince Philip.

'Who the 'ell would want a pair of pigeons on their mantle-piece?' was Windy's response, which I chose to disregard.

Although of no great age, they were valuable and had a strong following amongst collectors. I had always felt that the limited edition market could be fragile, but when the market was flying some years back, we had sold a set for just over £15,000, so I was quite excited.

'Fifteen grand for bloody pigeons?' spluttered Windy, when I told him what they were.

I decided I should tell the 'Really? Is that all?' lady, as I had given her nothing but bad news, and I thought some good news was called for. If I was expecting a positive reaction, I was disappointed. 'Oh' was all I got and she told me that her father had taken them in payment of a bad debt. The market for these had dipped, but they should still make around £5,000, which I thought was not a bad result, but my client seemed more concerned that the rest of the reproduction stuff from the house was going to make next to nothing.

I decided to go and see how my father was getting on and the answer was quite well. He was in the warm, my mother was nowhere near him, and he was guaranteed to get paid. I think sorting all the lots appealed to his inquisitive nature, in particular when he came across the company filing cabinet with correspondence from lawyers threatening court action. It was better than a soap opera for him.

The big thing to remember about bankrupt stock is that anything any good will have been sold in the final days of trading. In the literal sense, this was a liquidation sale not a bankrupt one – private individuals become bankrupt and companies go into liquidation – and this was a limited company that had got into financial difficulties, which resulted in the directors calling in the liquidator.

There was a great deal of bed linen amongst the stock that was 'interesting', to say the least. It was either so bright in colour that you would need to go to bed with sunglasses on, or was jet black with silver lurex figures in compromising positions. I could see why neither had set the marketplace alight. I chatted with my father about how we were going to get rid of the stock and we decided that a sale by tender would be the best method. This involved lotting the sale up like an auction, but then after viewing there would be a specified deadline by when interested parties could make bids.

There was an absolute mountain of stuff and, given all the colours, it looked like an explosion in a paint factory. Never mind, my father was happy tying together huge bundles of linen with baler twine. His baler twine was to become the trade mark of my father's new career – give him an opportunity to lash stuff together and out would come the twine and a pocket knife so sharp you could split a blade of grass with it. I decided the best course of action was to leave him to it, go back to the office, and place some adverts in *Exchange and Mart* and any other magazines I thought might be suitable for the linen tender sale.

I walked into the saleroom and was met by Windy.

''Ere, Phil, them pigeons. Coo . . . they should bring in a nice bill!'

He almost collapsed on the floor with what I thought might be a heart attack, but was in fact laughter. I simply stood there – it was clear when it came to sense of humour that Windy and I were on very different pieces of paper.

'See, Phil? Pigeons . . . billing and cooing?'

I thought it best to leave him to it, as further convulsions of merriment took over. I found a quiet corner in the saleroom and started to prepare the adverts for the linen job. Basically, this involved looking through old newspapers and *Exchange and Mart* and copying any advert that looked vaguely as if it did the trick. There were many firms of commercial auctioneers who did nothing other than this type of work, so I figured I wouldn't be far wrong if I cribbed their adverts.

I duly placed them and the next thing to do was get my hands on one of these firm's tender documents, so I could copy that as well. This reflected my approach to homework at school; my history essays were passed down from one academic year to the next, often for payment. I was quite pleased with everything, as I wanted to make sure we did a good job for my new father-in-law. Over the next few days, it was a question of sitting back and dealing with the interest and phone calls from linen buyers throughout the country. The viewing for the tender sale was in two weeks' time and the general sale was the day after, so it was all quite busy.

As the days went by, interest in the Sheet Sale was such that it became known in the office as the Sh*t Sale – the enquiries were limited to about eight phone calls and a couple of letters asking for tender forms. I was slipping into panic mode, but my father was very calm about it all, saying, 'You worry too much.' An observation that had a familiar ring to it.

I went into the saleroom before going to the tender sale to check that all was well. The doves were still out on the tables, so I asked Windy to put them somewhere safe.

'D'you reckon we'll have anybody who might fancy 'em?'

I knew what was coming, as Windy collapsed in another spasm of laughter.

'Pigeon fanciers, Phil! Geddit?'

It was time to go and look at the Sheet Sale.

I arrived at the warehouse to see a number of cars parked outside: most of them were posh German ones with personalised registration plates. I walked in and it was clear we weren't going to be pushed for room, as there were no more than fifteen people in the warehouse – all making copious notes. My father walked over and straight away I could see he was in his element; he had every bundle of linen stacked neatly in lot number order on tables.

If there was ever going to be a worldwide baler twine shortage, here was the man who would be responsible for it. The sheets and towels were tied up not once, but two or three times, and in the odd instance four times with orange twine. It was tied so tight, the viewers could barely see what was in each lot.

'Got to be careful. If they're not tight, we could get some nicked.'

Somehow or other, I didn't think we'd attracted an international ring of towel thieves and when I suggested we might notice someone walking out with a black king-size bed sheet with silver copulating couples on it, his response was, 'You can't trust no one.' I was going to point out that if you can't trust no one, you must be able to trust someone, but thought it might be wasted as an observation.

At that, one of the would-be buyers walked over and muttered, 'Can I have a word?' He ushered me into a corner of the warehouse. 'I was wondering if there was any incentive that I needed to offer?'

It must have been plain that I hadn't got the first idea what he was talking about. 'Cash incentive.' I was still none the wiser, so he pulled a roll of notes out of his pocket that would have cleared the debt of a small African country. 'How much?'

My father called me over.

'He wants to give you cash, a bung, to make sure he gets the lots he wants.'

I rushed back and hurriedly explained that we didn't work that way, and he should put his best price on the tender form and that would be that.

'Well, I just wanted to make sure we weren't out in the cold.'

I walked around the warehouse and spoke to some of the other viewers. It was like being in a scene from *Only Fools and Horses*; most of the would-be buyers were market traders who all knew one another and, without too much imagination, would have been right at home with Del Boy and Boycie in the Nag's Head, Peckham. I left my father and drove back to the saleroom to see how the viewing was going for the general sale.

It was funny, because whilst the two sales were wildly different in terms of the method of sale and what was being sold, the people were very similar. A lot of the buyers lived and worked in the shadows, and as far as some were concerned I think it fair to say that Her Majesty's Revenue and Customs staff would not have known of their existence; or perhaps more importantly, their business operations.

I could see Windy over the far side of the saleroom and walked over.

'The bloody pigeons fell off the branch!'

This was getting tiresome. I told Windy that a joke was a joke, but he was now scraping the barrel.

'No, Phil, I picked the box up and didn't realise it was loose. It tipped over and the bloody things fell off the branch. Just like someone had shot them stone dead.'

I looked in the box and sure enough the doves were lying in the box; the only damage was where they had become unglued and fallen off the branch. Windy must have dislodged something, but there was no point in blaming him. It was time to make the phone call that all auctioneers dread – telling a vendor that their prized possession has been damaged.

'Really?' she responded.

I was expecting that, but she was happy enough when I told her that the firm's insurance would pay her out mid-estimate. The insurance company paid out a cheque in the sum of £5,500 and I was left with the task of getting the model repaired, so it could be resold to recoup some of the payment.

My father enjoyed his time between the sheets, the result was good and all the buyers paid up with bankers' drafts and cash. He seemed to have found a niche for himself and supervised the whole job from start to finish. I spoke to Mr Hall about how the job had gone and he was delighted with the result, as was my firm, because it was profitable for us.

After a time spent trying to find a good restorer, I eventually got the doves reinstated on their branch. It was remarkable that they hadn't actually broken but appeared to have come away from the fixing. The restorer did such a good job that you would never know there had been a problem. Nonetheless, you could not sell them as perfect, because they weren't.

I rang the loss adjuster and told him what I thought they were now worth, which was about £1,500–2,500. The reply came back, 'Really – is that all?' A now-familiar phrase that brought a smile to my face. (They eventually sold for just under £2,000.)

Chapter 6

The Wonderful One

House clearances are a matter of sorting the wheat from the chaff and doing the best by the client. I got a call one day to go and look at the contents of a fairly ordinary house on the outskirts of Gloucester. On arrival, I was met by a lady who showed me round the property. It was her family who had clearly been well to do and a quick glance suggested that they had done a fair bit of travelling in their time. This was a house that had more than its fair share of wheat and even the chaff was going to be saleable. Everywhere you looked there were interesting lots from family portraits and miniatures to porcelain, silver, furniture and the catch-all term – *objets d'art*.

There was a lovely old mother-of-pearl bowl that fell into this last category – in truth, I didn't know what it was or how much it was worth, but I suggested it might make £300–500. I think that was a guesstimate, rather than an informed estimate. The lady client told me that the family had always believed it was a good thing, so I was happy I'd spotted it. I met Big Nige to clear the house and prepare a receipt form for the items we were removing, together with my suggested reserves and estimates.

People often get confused with reserves and estimates – put simply, a reserve is a price below which you won't sell a lot, and an estimate is what you expect it to make. It contravenes all rules and regulations to have a reserve higher than the bottom estimate, as a lot has to be able to be sold at the bottom figure. That said, there is a certain amount of psychology to estimates in the same way as a shop will price things to encourage the buyer; the old 19 shillings and 11 pence, or 99 new pence if you're not of a certain age, being prime examples.

The mother-of-pearl bowl was a conundrum for me; I was guessing what it was, how old it was and what it was worth. Nigel took the bigger lots back to the saleroom in his van and the smaller bits including the bowl made it back in my car. I carefully unpacked everything and laid it out on the tables. Windy offered to help, but I declined his offer on the grounds that I didn't want anything damaged and I certainly didn't want any more of his pigeon humour.

The more I looked at the mother-of-pearl bowl, the more I thought it might be something half decent. I decided not to put it into the next sale, but hold it back and do some research on it. The viewing for the next sale with the rest of the house contents was very encouraging; it looked as though all the lots would do well.

Viewing days were always a theatrical occasion, in the way that everyone had a role to play. The dealers inspected the lots they were interested in, and sometimes the lots they were not interested in to throw others, and the auctioneer, off the scent. Statements were made and you were never quite sure if it was someone's opinion, or whether it was designed to mislead you. One dealer was so adept at making these off-the-cuff remarks that you could, as my father used to say, hear him whisper three fields away.

This was all part of the saleroom theatre. I once overheard a dealer telling another dealer how good a particular vase was, how the estimate on it was ridiculously low and that it would make a lot more. What he omitted to tell him was that he owned the vase.

The first tranche of lots from the house sold well and made the money that fresh-to-the-market goods always do. I rang up my lady client to tell her how pleased I was. She too was delighted, as all my estimates had been comfortably exceeded; the conversation ended with, 'Have you had any more thoughts about the mother-of-pearl bowl?'

I'd had lots of thoughts, but none of them led to a conclusion – it was still sitting on a shelf in the store at the back of the saleroom. The problem with this approach was that it had turned into a case of out of sight, out of mind. Two, three, four and then five sales came and went and it was still sitting on the same shelf, getting a little bigger with the amount of dust it was gathering.

There is a point in your career when you think you've got it nailed and are reasonably confident with your knowledge. That doesn't last long, as reality creeps in and you realise there are huge gaps; it was a case of the more you knew, you realised the less you knew. I had a longing to learn more and a daunting realisation that I could never hope to compete with some of the specialist dealers who came to the saleroom.

Most weekends, Rose and I tried to do something or go somewhere – we were very lucky in that we shared common interests, so a trip to see a country house with a good collection of antiques was normally on the agenda. These trips would be combined with visits to any shops in the area; I was now getting to know most of the good antique shops, as many of their owners frequented the saleroom.

A trip to Bath resulted in a stop at the shop of very good dealer who stocked a wide range of quality antiques. Rose and I went into the shop and after a look around – a great way to learn is to handle pieces – we were invited into the inner sanctum of the back office. I loved these rooms: the office desk, which was usually a Georgian one, was normally cluttered with great items the shop owners couldn't bear to sell. This was no different; the desk was covered in small but highly collectable Grand Tour-type objects.

When the great and the good toured Europe at the end of the eighteenth and beginning of the nineteenth centuries, they brought back with them souvenirs of their trips. These could range from Italian furniture or paintings of Vesuvius to small marble statues in the classical style. This desk was littered with an eclectic mix of bronze lions, agate seals and small marble busts – in this instance, not memories of grand holidays, but of successful buying trips. There were bookcases all around the walls of the office, which were stacked with reference books and catalogues covering a huge range of subjects. Most good dealers had a reference library they could rely on to research the rarer lots that they bought.

Many antiques dealers are keen to discuss their stock and share their knowledge; we sat there chatting about how the market was strong in certain areas and what the trend might be in the coming months. Rose and the dealer were discussing Victorian furniture, when I was instantly drawn to a book that was on the table. I was miles away when I heard Rose saying, 'Phil, Phil – what do you think?'

I didn't think anything. I was staring at the book on the table, because on the back cover was a mother-of-pearl bowl. It was exactly the same as mine.

'We've lost you completely,' Rose went on.

She was right, I hadn't heard a word they were saying. I asked if I could have a look at the book.

'If you've got one of those, you're cooking on gas, Phil!'

I picked the book up and the description said the bowl illustrated was made in the Indian region of Gujurat in the late sixteenth or early seventeenth century. Apparently a lot of these were commissioned by Portuguese merchants as they travelled the East. Many of them were religious vessels and were made of small mother-of-pearl panels held in place by pins. I was pretty sure I now knew what it was, but I was still in the dark when it came to value.

'Not really my field, Phil, haven't seen one for years, let alone held one in stock. As rare as hen's teeth.' At least I had made some progress.

I spent the rest of the weekend thinking about the bowl; I had met a top London dealer who dealt in Eastern objects. I made up my mind that I would give him a call first thing on Monday morning to see if he could help me.

'Morning, Phil – when we selling that Pearl's mother's bowl?'

Windy didn't always grasp the finer points of the business, but was a dab hand at moving boxes and humping wardrobes. I was now spending so much time in his company that his personal problem went unnoticed by me, and by him. The only time it became an issue was when other people were around. This came to a head – or a bottom – when Windy and I were helping a lady unpack some boxes that she had brought in. After taking her details, we went across to the tables.

'I don't think there's anything of great value in the boxes. Please just sell them for me.'

As we walked across, Windy did what Windy did; for some reason I became hugely embarrassed and could feel myself going redder by the minute. The lady client gave me what my mother called an old-fashioned look. If it was a look designed to halt the pooping, it didn't. I think the fact that I reacted and not Windy reinforced her view that I was the culprit. As we were carrying the last box across the saleroom, Windy trumped all his previous efforts with an explosion that would have made a bull elephant proud. I went scarlet. The lady client looked at me and said in a loud voice, 'Well, really!' and walked out of the saleroom, never to be seen again.

It was time to apply my mind to the bowl. I telephoned the London dealer and told him what I thought I had, and asked him if I could send him some photos of the bowl for an opinion. Time had moved on and we were now in the world of the internet. In my view, this has been one of the biggest advances in the auctioneering world. We were able to send images all around the world, our sales could be advertised internationally and, more importantly, buyers from around the world were able to bid live at auctions by using various internet bidding platforms.

We had entered a click-and-collect world, where bidders bought lots they had seen only in images – relying on auctioneers to provide them with accurate condition reports on which they based their bids. There was a growing trend that fewer and fewer people attended auctions to bid in person, but chose to place their bids either online, or by bidding on the telephone. It was a far cry from the days when I first started with Mr Rayer. Preparing hand-written accounts with carbon paper and paying for lots with wads of ten-pound notes was now a thing of the past; we were in the age of glossy catalogues and settling accounts by bank transfer.

It was obvious that time had also moved on for Mr Rayer and he was involved much less with the business. He had been an inspiration to me; he never claimed to be the font of all knowledge, but he always put his clients' interests first and never expected any sympathy for his disability. He still retained an office and a core of his old clients, but he was now part-time. It was coming towards the end of an era; he had gone above and beyond the call of duty with me, and had been the guiding light in my career.

'Phil, there's some bloke on the phone wants to talk to you about an Indian bowl. He might have been drinking – sounded like he said Bergerac, that detective bloke. You'd better have a word. I don't know what he's on about.'

It was the London dealer.

'Philip, that is a good bowl – definitely Gujurat and probably somewhere between 1580 and 1620.' He confirmed that wealthy Portuguese travellers and merchants had stopped in this region of India to have religious vessels made by local craftsmen. He told me that the bowl would probably have had a ewer with it. He added that at about eighteen inches in diameter, my bowl was bigger than most of the ones he had seen in the past.

'Should make fifteen to twenty.' He was clearly not referring to pounds. 'I'd put a reserve on it of about £12,000. I think if you get much over the £20,000 mark, you'll have done your client proud and over twenty-five, you'll have swum the channel. Book me a phone line, please.'

It was all short and to the point and very encouraging that he was keen to bid on it. I had managed to find this out only through the chance sighting of a book in Bath and the generous imparting of knowledge from the dealer in London.

I was keen to let my client know the good news. 'In the family we had always been led to believe it was a good thing, Philip, but we hadn't realised it was that good.'

Through the passage of time, family rumours can become a little enhanced and glorified; the number of times that Nelson's snuff box ends up being a small wooden box made in the Lancashire town of Nelson were too numerous to mention. In this instance, family folklore had been more than justified. I advertised the bowl in the specialist trade newspaper, and before the sale we had a huge amount of interest from all over the world. There was no doubt that the internet was proving its worth, and there was another lot in the sale that I thought would benefit from similar exposure.

I have always believed that we hark back to our youth when we start to collect. In my own youth, there was a musical revolution with new pop groups such as The Beatles and the Rolling Stones. Their music influenced a whole generation of teenagers, of which I was one. Autographs of these bands have become very collectable and in the Bergerac sale – as it was now known – I had been asked to include a scrap of paper signed by John, Paul, George and Ringo. A gentleman client had seen them when they came to Worcester and had got their autographs after the show.

We discussed value and suffice to say that his expectations were punchy in the extreme, as he had seen their signatures advertised for a lot of money. These weren't going to be sold for nothing, but I had no doubt that the right person would pay the right price. Provenance is everything to these things and when I asked the gentleman how he got them, he told me he had queued at the stage show and given them the piece of paper to sign. No problem there then – or so I thought. I was building up quite a network of dealer friends and one of them specialised in pop memorabilia generally, and The Beatles and their signatures in particular. He was passing the saleroom *en route* to another auction and I showed him the signatures, thinking that it would whet his appetite for the forthcoming sale.

'Well, Phil, these things aren't always obvious.'

I wasn't sure I liked the sound of that; I sensed that bad news was about to follow. 'Sometimes they all signed their signatures, sometimes John or Paul did them, and sometimes their roadie signed them. Or a combination of all of those!'

I told him that my client had actually seen them sign it.

'They all say that, Phil.'

I needed to know how many of mine were signed originally by all four of the band.

'Sorry, Phil,' was not the portent of good news. He was of the view that two of them were signed by the band and two were signed by the roadie. This reduced the value considerably and as my client wanted a full price for them, this was going to cause a problem. I was at a bit of a loss, as my client was adamant that he handed the boys the bit of paper outside the theatre door in Worcester in the early 1960s. I gave him a call and asked him to come into the saleroom.

'Honestly, after the show I waited outside the backstage door – as you can imagine, Beatlemania was taking off and there was a lot of us. I was at the front of the queue and didn't have an autograph book, so I handed them my piece of paper to sign.'

I understood that, but I needed to know if he had seen them sign it themselves.

'I handed it to John.' This was old ground, but had they all signed it? 'Well, he went inside with lots of other bits of paper and books and came out with them ten minutes later.'

It was hard work, but I was gradually getting there.

'So I didn't actually see them sign it, but I mean who else would have signed it?'

I gently broke it to him that only two of the signatures were original and as such the value was considerably reduced.

'Well, wouldn't it be more of a collector's item?'

I think he was grasping at straws now – collectors of The Beatles autographs wanted John, Paul, George and Ringo, not John, Paul, Kevin and Trevor, or whoever it was. I explained that this had a serious impact on their value.

'Well, if that's all you think they're worth, I'll have them back.' I got the feeling that he didn't believe what I was telling him, and they might find their way onto the market with no mention as to authenticity.

I might not have had the Fab Four in the sale, but I still had the Wonderful One – in the shape of my Gujurat bowl. The interest created by the bowl was as strong as any lot we had sold recently; the internet had done its job with the number of enquiries. Come the sale day, there were ten telephone lines booked by bidders from all over the globe, so it was looking good.

I walked into the office and saw that we had received an email from another client who wanted to bid by phone. I had to email back and tell him we were clean out of phones, which meant he could leave a commission for us to bid on his behalf, or he could bid online. He chose the latter, which meant that he could keep his powder dry by not letting me know what he thought it was worth. I wasn't sure where he was calling from, but got the impression he was a European dealer specialising in these type of objects.

There's always an air of excitement in the saleroom when a good lot is about to be sold and there was definitely a bowl buzz going on. I was going to be in charge of the gavel when it was offered, so I made my way to the rostrum about twenty lots before, secretly hoping that it would hit the £20,000 mark.

The bidding opened at £10,000 and quickly rose to £21,000, with all the telephone lines competing against one another. At £30,000 the bidding was between three telephone lines; on it went to £46,000, when one of the phone bidders decided that was enough. At £52,000 the second phone bidder dropped out and I was about to bring the gavel down when the internet suddenly lit up; I assumed that it was the dealer who I had been in email contact with earlier who was bidding online.

The telephone bidder was from across the pond and suddenly Malvern had entered the international art world. It eventually sold for £77,000 and my client was overjoyed.

The next day my London dealer friend called to tell me how well he thought the sale had gone. Frankly, it was in no small part down to his help, and I was very aware of that.

'Phil – it's your old college on the phone.'

It had been some years since I had left Loughborough College of Physical Education. I didn't think I had an outstanding bar bill, but they were after me for something.

'Philip, it's Veronica from Loughborough here. We need your advice.'

These were words I never thought I'd hear. It's funny the twists and turns that life takes. When I went to Loughborough to study PE and Geography, as far as I was concerned it was the best PE college in the country and I was hugely proud then, and still am now, to have got in there.

There was life at Loughborough other than being a 'Jock' (a PE student) and, if I had taken the time to consider it, I would have known that you could also go there to become a 'Chippy' – these were the guys who studied the Creative Design course. Not strictly true, but essentially Jocks ran around all day in purple track suits and Chippies made things out of wood. If I had paid more attention to the heritage of the Chippies, I would have realised that Loughborough has a significant history in that regard, too.

'Philip, we've got a load of wardrobes and chests in a warehouse that we think might be worth something. They were made by the students.'

My initial reaction was that Mr Thomas Chippendale had nothing to worry about. However, I was aware now that Loughborough was significant in the Arts and Crafts movement. These were a group of artists and craftsmen who wanted to move away from the industrialisation of the mid-nineteenth century and concentrate more on revealing the method of construction. The traditional method of constructing a chest of drawers involved hiding the dovetails, but the movement exposed the dovetails, so they were visible and became a feature of the design. There was a large Arts and Crafts movement in Gloucestershire, where Peter Waals and Edward Barnsley had been leading exponents specialising in the design of furniture.

You never know what to expect, so I made an appointment to drive back to my old haunts of a misspent youth and see what the university wanted to sell. I drove past a big pair of iron gates, which brought a smile to my face. As a schoolboy catching the train for an interview at the college, I arrived in Loughborough and had no idea where I was going, so I stopped to ask the local postman.

'It's up by the bastard gates, m'duck.'

I don't know what had upset him, but the way he called me

'm'duck' was a little unnerving. I stopped to ask a lady walking her dog. 'Yes, m'duck. Carry on this road and turn left through the bastard gates.' These gates must have upset a large number of people.

I reported in for my interview and the lady enquired if I'd had any problems getting there. I mentioned the 'gate' conversations and asked why they were such a problem. The explanation cleared things up – apparently the former chairman of the governors was William Bastard and the gates were named after him. Pity his poor children, who must have been known as little Bastards.

For clarification, when I first went to Loughborough it was a PE college and after I left, the PE side became a department of the university. My entrance interview was geared to passing a rugby ball and throwing a cricket ball. Nowadays they have to do exams, which would have been a serious hurdle to me ever gaining admission.

I met Veronica and we went to the storage building where all the wardrobes and chests were held. 'There is a slight complication, Philip. We need to be out of here by the end of next month.'

As we opened the door, all I could see was a mountain of furniture that was so crammed in you could hardly get into the building and, at first glance, did not appear to have any great merit. Looks can be deceptive, however. Veronica explained, 'Peter Waals and Edward Barnsley were lecturers here and they designed furniture for the students' rooms; the Creative Design students then had to make it under their supervision.'

She showed me photographs: all of the units were basically the same, with a single-door wardrobe next to a chest of drawers, both sitting on a plinth, whilst some had a small shelf unit over the chest. The knobs and handles all differed slightly, but in essence they were the same.

'We hadn't realised they were here and the building has to be emptied. I think the workmen were just going to skip it all, but we thought you might be able to raise some money for us?'

There was so much stuff in the warehouse, you couldn't tell a bee from a bull's foot. She went on, 'I can get it all moved into one of the halls short-term, so at least you can see it and sell it.' It was a step in the right direction, and I made an appointment to come back in a week's time to work out the best thing to do with it all.

On my return, the units were all neatly laid out in rows like soldiers awaiting inspection in one of the university halls. As I walked around, it brought back memories of my student days, as I'd had one of these units in my room. It also struck me as a very clever move on the part of the university to get the students to make furniture for their own rooms, and then mark them on it as part of the course work.

There weren't that many complete units and it was also pretty obvious that there was a vast range in the quality of the goods that were made, particularly the mirrors. I'm not sure what grade was given to the student who made the unit in my room, but I wouldn't be surprised if he was thrown off the course. I walked around the hall opening various drawers, looking for one that had 'Phil was here' written in it, but I was sadly disappointed.

The furniture did have a look – as it should, given its design origins – and I could see there would be a demand for it. The problems facing me were the lack of complete units and the fact that the sale was very niche, meaning if you weren't into Arts and Crafts or Loughborough, it wasn't for you. Most importantly, there was a time and space issue, as the university wanted its hall back. I'd like to say it was my idea, though I'd be lying, but one of the 'Loughborough Ladies', who dealt with the university alumni, suggested that we should contact former students who might like to buy a memento of their student days.

As time was an issue, I decided to catalogue the sale there and then: Lot 1 – A wardrobe unit; Lot 2 – ditto; Lot 3 – ditto, and on it went until we got to the mirrors, which were dealt with in a similar manner – a lot of dittos. The final lot I catalogued was a good, round oak table that I didn't see on my first visit, as it had been hidden by the wardrobe units. It looked to be of far better quality than the rest, which wasn't the greatest compliment, but I thought it was probably the best of a bad lot.

To be truthful, most of the furniture did not look to be worth a huge amount and I was beginning to worry that I was giving the university bad advice. A lot of the units had bits missing and many did not match properly. The university was spending money moving the lots around the campus, and if you added that to the sale costs, I wondered if there would be anything left over. I was told that any proceeds we made would be for the benefit of the students and the last thing I wanted was to cost them money.

We weren't exactly bowled over with enquiries for the Loughborough sale and as Jim eloquently pointed out to me in the Greyhound, 'Who the hell wants a wardrobe and chest of drawers knocked up by a load of students? They were probably drunk when they made the stuff.'

I had now convinced myself that the right advice would have been for them not to incur any further expenditure, cut their losses and dump the lot. I was in full-on Serrell panic mode. We drove up to Loughborough the night before the auction and stayed in student rooms. Looking around the room that the university had put me in, I wondered if in years to come the metal wardrobe and chipboard chest of drawers would have any value at auction – I doubted it.

I made my way to the saleroom and was pleasantly surprised to be told we had over 100 people registered to bid online; there were a number of former students and some of my old lecturers had also registered, who were in the room. The question was, were they there to bid or to 'kick tyres'? Well, the answer was bid – and bid they did. The best wardrobe unit sold for over £800 and the smart oak table that was the last lot in the sale took £3,400; by the time we had finished selling everything, we had taken just over £40,000.

Veronica came up to me afterwards.

'We're so grateful, Philip – you gave us just the advice we needed. There were times when we thought you'd got it wrong and we should have dumped it all, but you were right.'

Never in doubt, was it?

Chapter 7

Prime Suspect

My auction world was getting more diverse with student-made wardrobes and a warehouse full of dodgy sheets – they say variety is the spice of life. I was wondering what would come up next as I drove out towards Ledbury to look at a small collection of Worcester porcelain that a family wanted me to see. I had spoken to the daughter on the phone, who told me that the collection was her mother's and whilst her mother wanted to sell it, the daughter was quite against it being sold.

It was a cold day as I drove through Ledbury and eventually came to my destination; a remote cottage at the far end of a country lane full of potholes. Some houses have a warm feeling and some have a cold one; this place would have had Eskimos shivering. From the outside the house looked cold, and the grey pebble-dashed walls and the roof of corrugated iron sheets did nothing to allay this feeling.

I stood in the glazed lean-to porch; a very apt description since it was doing exactly that – leaning to. The panes of glass were mostly cracked and I knocked on the dark green painted door. A lady of about fifty appeared. 'Could I have a word, please, before we see Mum?'

I was fine with that, but wanted to get inside as it was

wretchedly cold; it probably wasn't that cold, but it was the way I was feeling.

'The porcelain is a family heirloom. I don't really want her to sell it – she will just spend the money and then it'll all be gone.'

I've said it before, 'Where there's a will, there's a relative,' except in this case the mother was still very much alive.

We walked into the sitting room, where there was a lady whom I imagine was aged about eighty. She was sitting with her coat on around a fire that was giving out marginally less heat than a spent match.

'Thank you for coming. I'm thinking of selling the china on the shelves by the window, but my daughter doesn't want me to.' The daughter interrupted, 'It would be a pity to sell it after all this time; it's been in the family nearly 150 years.'

There were three vases and two plates decorated with sheep by one of the greatest ceramic painters of the twentieth century. Harry Davis was the artist and his work is instantly recognisable. I tried to point out delicately that it couldn't have been in the family for that length of time, when the daughter butted in again. 'Mr Serrell, even you experts are wrong sometimes. I know it's been in the family for that long.'

The Royal Worcester porcelain factory used a date code that they put on the bottom of their vases and plates. By simply looking at the codes on these pieces, I could see they dated from the mid-1920s, so I knew I was right; not that it mattered to the daughter.

'That date must be wrong, because I know we've had them that long. They're an heirloom.' I pointed out to her that as Harry was born in 1885, it was unlikely he was so talented that he could have painted them before he was born.

'Well, I don't want her to sell them. I know it's just about the money to you.'

The words pot and kettle sprang to mind.

Her mother looked confused and not a little hurt. She told me that if she could sell her porcelain for a few thousand pounds, which is what she thought it was worth, she could spend it on making her life a little more comfortable. She was also frightened that she might knock them over and as the contents of her home weren't insured, she would get nothing if she did break them.

I looked around the room. It was very shy of creature comforts; it was both cold and damp and the porch windows weren't the only ones that were cracked. Most of the panes in the window by the china were in a poor state and were covered in her homespun attempt at double glazing – cellophane and plastic held in by yellowing Sellotape.

The daughter then left the room to make herself a cup of tea. Her mother and I weren't asked if we wanted one, which was fine for me, but I felt for her mother. Whilst she was out of the room, her mother told me that her daughter didn't want her to sell anything as it would be less for her to inherit. At that, the daughter came back into the room and I brought up the subject of insurance. This was an issue that concerned me, as from a security point of view the house was like a sieve; you could have leaned on the front door or any of the windows to break in.

'Waste of money,' replied the daughter. I pointed out that if her mother was worried about damaging the vases, she really should insure them. It was a tricky situation, as I was worried about burglary, but didn't want to frighten the old lady.

'No need – she only goes out to collect on pension day. Anyway, what are they worth?' I thought the three vases might be worth about £1,500 each and the plates about £250 each, so all in all about £5,000. This produced an interesting insight into human nature. The mother said, 'Really, as much as that?' and the daughter said, 'Is that all?', a phrase I had heard many times before.

It was pretty obvious to me that there was no way the Worcester would be sold, as the daughter ruled her mother with a rod of iron and she wasn't going to loosen her grip on her inheritance. I bade my farewells, but stressed to them both that at the very least they should make sure the pots were insured. It was too much of a risk in case they got damaged or, even worse, stolen.

As I made my way back to the saleroom, I kept thinking about Worcester Porcelain Cottage and the lady who lived there. It was really sad, but I came to the conclusion that everyone had to live their own life and whatever I felt, it was unlikely to change things. When I got to the saleroom, Big Nige had been in and Windy had unpacked boxes from another house clearance. Clearing someone's home was a job that you had to be fairly blasé about; if you stopped to think that it was people's lives you were dealing with, it could get to you.

It was easy to be judgmental about what people had bought or collected, if not sometimes a little pompous. The current boxes had come from a retired military man, whose family had been in the forces for generations before him. It was clear from the boxes that Windy had unpacked that several generations ago the family had spent time in China and Japan. There were a lot of decorative vases and general trinkets, which would have been bought from markets and stalls in the Orient at the turn of the last century. Nothing looked overly special to me, and Windy had done a good job laying it all out on the table tops ready for me to group into boxes in suitable lots.

These boxes were the staple diet of the general sales and were bought by dealers – full and part-time – who had stalls at the various antique fairs and markets. There is an old story of two antique dealers with a silver dish on a desert island, who made a living for ten years selling it back and forth to one another. The auctions and markets were part of that cycle. I couldn't face sorting through it all at that moment; give me a chance to put something off and I will. So I did.

It was a good job that I had. A week later, I was in the saleroom when a London dealer called in and asked if he could have a look around as he was passing through. Big Nige was in the saleroom and my role was reduced to making them both a cup of coffee.

'Any biccies, Phil?'

I wandered over to the dealer, who was trawling through the oriental bits on the end of one of the tables. One particular vase had captured his interest more than the others.

'Is this in your next sale?'

It was a small cloisonné vase decorated with birds and flowers about six inches high. Cloisonné is a technique where a metal ornament has wires applied to its surface to create compartments that are then infilled with enamel pastes and fired; the wires stop the colours from running into one another.

'Don't suppose you've got the cover for it?'

'No,' said Windy.

'Yes,' said Big Nige.

'Well, it's pretty crucial,' said the dealer. 'Makes a tump of difference to the price. I may as well tell you, it's by a Japanese man called Namikawa Yasuyuki.' In all honesty, I was none the wiser. 'It's from the Meiji Period,' which I knew was from the late 1860s to before the start of the First World War. 'I'd normally have said nothing and just come back and bought it, but I'd far rather have it with the cover than without it. Here's my number – let me know how you get on finding it.'

Big Nige was adamant it was in the house and had been packed up by him, just as Windy was equally adamant that he had not unpacked it in the saleroom.

'Must still be in the boxes,' was Big Nige's answer to the problem. We went to the storeroom and were confronted by the European cardboard box mountain, and each box was full of newspaper.

'It'll be in one of them,' was Nige's astute observation, followed by Windy's equally astute, 'Bugger me – and I'm going to have to go through them all to find it.'

I left Windy to start the task of going through box after box of old newspapers. I thought it best to keep out of the way, so I left him to it over the next few days, occasionally popping in to see if he had found it.

'Look at me 'ands, Phil – looks like I've been down a coal pit!'

After about a week, I called into the saleroom and was greeted by an elated Windy running towards me across the saleroom with the inevitable consequences. His arm was outstretched with his hand holding a small cover about half an inch in height. It wasn't often, if ever, that I felt the urge to hug Windy, but this was probably the closest I'd ever come to it. I rang the dealer to tell him we'd found the cover.

'Book me a phone line, please, Philip.'

The sale day duly arrived. One of the local specialist dealers came up to me and said, 'How the hell did you know who that vase was by?' I fleetingly toyed with idea of telling him it had been the subject of painstaking research, but decided to tell him the truth. 'Well, it's either going to cost him, or me, a lot of money,' he laughed.

When the lot came up, I wasn't on the rostrum but on the telephone to the London dealer. 'Much interest, Philip, or am I going to nick it?' As such there was no reserve on the vase, because it had come from a deceased estate house clearance, but I still wanted to try and get good money for it. I wasn't sure what it was worth, but thought a £600–900 estimate was sensible. The bidding in the room opened at £500 and crept up to just under the £2,000 mark, when it became a straight contest between the local dealer and my man on the telephone.

Eventually the gavel came down in my favour for the London man on the telephone at £13,000, blowing my estimate clean out of the water. As the dealer in the room walked past me, he said, 'Told you it would cost him, Philip. I'd have got it for nothing if it wasn't for him.' He was right, of course – but it wouldn't have had a cover.

The London man must have been delighted, because he was at the saleroom the next day to collect his vase and pay for it. I was equally delighted and even managed to find him the box and newspaper in which it had first come into the saleroom.

As he walked out of the saleroom with his cloisonné vase, one of the local policemen walked in. This was not an unusual occurrence, as they popped in fairly regularly on their rounds. In truth, it was something I encouraged – I always felt it was good to be on the right side of the law.

'Fancy a coffee, Andy?'

'Thanks, Windy, but I'm here on official business. Phil, there's been a break-in at a cottage over in Ledbury. Bit embarrassing this, but the daughter seems to think you might have something to do it.'

I was absolutely flabbergasted. I have been accused of many things, but this was a first. Andy explained that the cottage had been broken into and the only things that had been stolen were the five pieces of Worcester porcelain. I pointed out that it was probably because there was nothing else worth pinching.

The daughter had apparently told the police that I was her prime suspect as I had been there recently, identified the Worcester in question and told her that I thought a burglary was a serious possibility. Not only that, but it had been stolen in broad daylight whilst the mother was out collecting her pension and the daughter had told me that it was the only day her mother was out of the house. Whoever had broken in had done so by forcing the window by the shelves on which the vases sat.

'Phil, I know it's not you, but the daughter said that you pointed out the dodgy window to her.'

I didn't know what to say or do.

'Look, don't worry, but because the daughter has made the suggestion, we have to follow it up as a line of enquiry.'

The whole situation made me feel very uncomfortable.

'Sad thing is, Phil, they didn't have any insurance.' He told me the mother was almost relieved that the pots weren't her problem any more, but the daughter was really angry – not that the vases and plates had gone, but as she said to Andy, 'Think of the money I've lost. I mean, we've lost.'

'We've got a chair in the car outside – it's a bit tatty, but we think it might be worth something. Could you come and have a look at it, please.'

The 'we' was an elderly lady and gentleman and their dress was more John Deere rather than Paul Smith. Not the most promising of opening gambits, but I followed them outside to the saleroom car park.

I hadn't seen the chair yet, but I wasn't sure whether the 'tatty' bit referred to the chair or their car. It was a seventeen-year-old Datsun estate car that could well have started out life brown in colour, but now it was hard to tell. It was covered in what I hoped was farmyard mud but, judging from the smell coming from the car, it could have been something far worse. It also had a rust problem – or the rust had a car problem – because there was probably more evidence of the tin worm than there was metal.

This was not promising; I tried to peer in through the tailgate window, but whatever was on it had set like concrete. It wasn't so much cleaning it needed, as sand blasting.

'Let me,' the man said. 'I hope we're not wasting your time.'

He opened the tailgate and took out a chair covered in a blanket. He closed the tailgate very gently and I could see why, because as it shut a shower of sand-like rust dropped in a line where it was parked. I wouldn't want to go on a long journey in the car; far less of it would arrive at the destination than when you started.

As he took the blanket off the chair, I was expecting a Victorian carved-oak monstrosity and was preparing my speech of how this was not a good time to sell it. The best thing to do would be to hang on to it and hopefully it would grow into a bit of money, if they kept it for about three hundred years.

'It belonged to our grandmother, so we know it's got a bit of age.'

There is a common fallacy in the antique world that anything that belonged to a grandmother is both old and valuable. It's not. As the blanket came off the chair, I could see I was some way off the mark with my guess at a Victorian monstrosity. It was a wonderful eighteenth-century armchair dating to around 1735–1745.

My first concern was that woodworm – a distant cousin of the Datsun's tin worm – had not attacked the chair. It hadn't, but it also hadn't seen a coat of polish since about 1746. That was not necessarily a bad thing; the worst thing you can do to any piece of furniture is to strip it clean and take off all depth of colour and patination. When the good Lord invented wire wool and sandpaper, he didn't do the antique trade a lot of favours.

At least the frame was sound, which was more than could be said for the seat. It was covered in a type of tapestry that was probably original, but looked as if it had been attacked by a flail. I struggled to hide my gaze from the seat.

'It was where the cat used to sharpen its claws.' This was a moggy I would not want to get on the wrong side of. 'If it's not worth anything, we can take it away, but the truth is we need to raise some money.'

It was a fine chair, of that I had no doubt, and I was sure it would do well at auction, though examples as good as this didn't turn up every day of the week in my saleroom. I asked them how much they hoped to raise.

'Well, we're not really sure, but we'd like to get over five thousand if we could.' That didn't seem unreasonable to me; I was sure it was a good thing and should do that sum without too much difficulty.

I took the chair into the saleroom and filled out the necessary paperwork, and told them I would try to come up with a more definite figure in terms of value.

'Bloody 'ell, Phil, what's that old chair. Are we that desperate for stuff?' was Windy's way of questioning my judgement. 'And what the 'ell's 'appened to the seat? Looks like somebody's 'ad a go at it with a razor. Good job it's not worth much.'

That last remark didn't do much for the fragile Serrell confidence. I told Windy I thought it was actually quite a good chair, that the clients were hoping for upwards of £5,000 and the seat was that way because of the family moggy sharpening its claws.

'Five grand for a cat chair – you've lost it this time, Phil.'

I showed the chair to a number of dealers, who all said, 'Good chair, that,' or something similar, which told me what I already knew but not much else. My trusty saleroom porter kept muttering to anyone who would listen to him, 'Look at the seat on that chair – five grand, he's told 'em. 'E's lost it this time. Bloody cat chair.'

It was at this point I thought it best to move the chair into the store, if for no other reason than to save me from the constant barrage of Windy's expert advice. I figured that out of sight, out of a mind was a good adage to adopt in these circumstances.

I was enjoying the very tiny cottage that Rose and I had bought and we were slowly furnishing it. It was in one of the timbered Worcestershire villages that adorn many postcards. Money was beyond tight; like most young couples, no matter how we did the sums, there seemed to be a shortfall on the mortgage every month. We came to the conclusion it was best to ignore money, as we always seemed to get there. A lot of our furniture came from saleroom cast-offs that buyers left behind. Our settee was part of a three-piece suite that someone had discarded, because they only wanted the two armchairs that came with it. The fact that the two-seat sofa had only one cushion may have had something to do with it.

Rose's answer was to make a cushion out of old sheets, which I filled with hay, and she covered the whole ensemble with a loose throw. I don't think anyone was ever the wiser, though I was anxious in case anyone came to visit who was a hay-fever sufferer.

I also had to make sure that if we did have guests – other than Jim, who didn't count – that I was the one who sat on it. It was at this time that Rose wanted a puppy; I suppose it could have been worse. I had always wanted a dog, but my mother had forbidden it on the grounds that it was something else to look after and it would be messy. She most definitely did not want one in the house – she thought my father was trouble enough.

Rose had always had animals, but I was worried as to who would look after it during the day. Eventually it was decided that we would get a Jack Russell terrier puppy that would come to work with me and I would walk it during the day.

'What's 'is name?' was Windy's first question – sharp as a new pin was Windy, as I pointed out that Worm was a 'her' and not a 'him', and she was so-called because she used to eat worms in the garden.

'Worm, what sort of name's that and who's gonna walk who, Phil?' was his response when I told him that I was going to take her up the Malvern Hills whenever I could. 'We'll put 'im on the bloody cat chair – 'e'll have somewhere to sit!' He had chosen to ignore the 'she' bit. It occurred to me again that humour is a very strange thing, as Windy vanished over to the other side of the saleroom chuckling at his own 'joke'.

Having mentioned the chair, I went into the storeroom and had another look at it to see if any further divine inspiration was going to hit me. Worm followed me through the sale-room. She was very much becoming the saleroom dog; though I had to stop Windy from feeding her biscuits.

I decided I would give the vendors a phone call to see if they could give me any information as to the history of the chair; some sort of provenance might help, if there was any. It was a fruitless telephone call that drew a complete blank; they had no idea where it had come from. I thought that was going to be the end of the conversation, but it wasn't.

'Mr Serrell, it's a bit embarrassing, but . . .,' my experience of life was that whenever there was a 'but', it was followed by bad news, '. . . we need it to be sold as soon as possible really – in fact in the next sale, please.' That wasn't a bad 'but', though it became clear that it still wasn't all. 'If you're happy to do so, we'd like you to write a letter to us confirming the reserve will be five thousand pounds.'

As the conversation went on, they told me they had an overdraft at the bank, which the proceeds of sale would go to paying off, and their bank manager wanted some confirmation from the auctioneers that funds would be forthcoming from the sale that would cover it. I explained that whilst I couldn't guarantee anything, I would be happy to confirm that the chair would be going into an auction with a £5,000 reserve.

Worm and I went out to the car and set off for our next appointment – well, that's what I told Windy – the reality was we set off for a walk up the Malvern Hills. It was a breezy day and a good walk up to the Beacon was a great way of me gathering my thoughts. Whenever I wanted to have a bit of peace and quiet, I took to the Hills with Worm. She didn't make too much contribution to my thoughts about eighteenth-century chairs, but she was a good listener.

Pre-sale interest in the chair was as good as I had hoped, with two dealers registering to bid on the telephone, and on the sale day there were a number of fresh faces in the room. A strange thing to say, and I've made reference to it before, but they dressed as if they had money; it's a thing that auctioneers get a sixth sense about. I'm not sure I can expand on that, but Windy summed it up better. 'Some fresh faces here today, Phil – faces with a tan that ain't out of a bottle and clothes that ain't out of a catalogue.'

I was always anxious before a big lot came up, but I was a little more so on this occasion. I hoped my letter to the bank manager wouldn't be taken as some sort of guarantee. I was now in total overdrive panic, as I could see a writ from the bank dropping on the mat when the chair failed to sell.

I had to concentrate as I heard myself say, 'Now ladies and gentlemen, the eighteenth-century mahogany armchair – bid me £5,000?'

Silence.

'£4,000 then?' A louder silence. 'Start me at £3,000?'

I could almost hear the bank manager beating the saleroom door down. All those in their smart clothes with supertanned faces simply stared at me.

Eventually one of the local dealers shouted out, 'A thousand, sir!'

I looked around the room – nothing – I then looked at the two girls on the phone lines. One gently shook her head and the other gave me a shrug of the shoulders. The bank manager had turned into the grim reaper complete with long cloak and scythe, and I could see me being drummed out of the firm.

'Anymore?' I scanned the room and after what seemed an eternity, one of the tanned ones put his hand up. 'Fifteen hundred, sir.'

His entrance into the fray seemed to spark other tanned ones into action and we shot up to £10,000 in bids of £500. I wasn't sure if any of them heard the audible sigh as we went past £5,000, but they must have been deaf if they didn't. At £15,500 the room bidding stopped and with the gavel about to come down, the first of the telephone bidders suddenly came alive and this was quickly followed by the second phone line up to £27,000, when it finally sold.

I was pleased, the client was happy and I would think the bank manager was delighted beyond his expectation – in fact beyond everyone's expectation. We were all pleased with the result at the saleroom, but Windy brought everyone down to earth with his own level of reality. 'Twenty-seven grand for a chair that a cat's ripped the seat out of. World's gone mad!' I left him to mutter to himself.

There was a postscript to this in that, sometime later when Rose and I were away for the weekend, we called into the shop of an upmarket dealer and saw 'The Cat Chair' in pride of place; the seat was now covered in a really lovely period tapestry fabric that was a huge improvement on the original cat-ravaged example. I was standing there looking at it when the delightful sales assistant wandered over to talk to me; a young lady whom I hadn't met before.

'Isn't that a gorgeous chair?' she said, 'and so very reasonably priced.'

I smiled as I walked out.

Chapter 8

The Chinese Vase and Indian Watch

Clients come in all shapes and sizes and the one standing in front of me was probably at the far end of the scale. She was a lady who appeared to have modelled herself on one of the characters in the 1980s TV series *Dynasty*, about the lives of the super-rich. Her suit wasn't quite Chanel – more like Canal – but the jacket did have the obligatory shoulder pads, which looked as if she had left the coat hanger in by mistake. Her make-up was so thick, it must have been applied using a spray gun and masking tape.

'Mr Serrell. I bought this table from another local sale-room. I wanted to turn it into a wash basin in my bathroom, but it's too wide.'

She went on to tell me that the table had cost her £130 and her plan was to get a local plumber to cut a hole in the top and drop a sink in; however, when she got it home the Edwardian table was too wide. What I did know was that it wasn't an Edwardian side table, but a Chinese altar table, and I guessed it was early nineteenth century at the latest and possibly eight-eenth century. If so, it was worth a good deal more than she had paid, but Dame Dynasty was very philosophical about it.

'As long as I get my £130 back, I shall be happy. I have an eye for these things.' She asked me to put a £130 reserve on it. 'Antiques aren't really my thing, but I'm sure someone will buy it. I have a sense of style and I'm sure other bidders will see what I see.'

Looking at the shoulder pads and make-up, it was clear that she had a sense of style, but I'm not sure it was a particularly good one. We agreed to put it into our next antique sale, which would also have a catalogue online, and she swept out of the saleroom with the parting remark, 'Mr Serrell, that little Edwardian table is going to light up someone's life.' I was going to point out that I didn't think it was Edwardian but I was too late, as she was back in her car checking her make-up in the rear view mirror.

Antiques are like buses. You wait for hours and don't see one, then you can't move for them, or perhaps more accurately, the people with antiques who want to sell them. On occasion there appears to be a theme for what comes into the saleroom and this one had an oriental flavour to it. I had a call from a lady who said she had a Chinese vase she wanted to sell, so I made an appointment to pop out and see her.

It was a glorious day as I set out over the Malvern Hills with the sun shining towards the Brecon Beacons. Many people prefer the east side of the hills, with its view over the River Severn towards Worcester and the Cotswolds, but I've always favoured the more rural west side with its landscape towards Hay Bluff, Herefordshire and the Welsh Marches.

That was the direction I was heading in today to a farm between Ledbury and Hereford, with Worm sitting on the passenger seat. I was lucky she seemed to enjoy the car and couldn't wait to get in when I set out for work in the morning. Trips like this always ensured that we could stop and take a walk in some of the most glorious countryside in the area.

The lady in question was from a Herefordshire farming family whom Mr Rayer had dealt with previously. I was excited, because it was a new contact for me, and her family had been well known and successful in the local farming world for three or four generations – the term 'old money' sprang to mind.

I was also pleased that one of Mr Rayer's clients had sought to call me out. Experience taught me that it was this type of family who had bought good things in the past and, in my eyes, this meant they might have good things to sell in the present. I was slightly nervous, though, because my knowledge of Chinese porcelain could be written on the back of a very small postage stamp; there was no point in trying to convince the lady to the contrary, as it would only turn around and bite me.

The lady I had come to see was almost the exact opposite of my previous client who owned the 'Edwardian table'; understated in the extreme. She had dark curly hair, a green Guernsey sweater, a pair of jeans and a pair of green wellingtons. That was pretty much the norm, but her hair looked as if she had cut it herself, her sweater had leather patches on old leather patches, her jeans were faded and torn in a way that sounded trendy but wasn't, and her wellingtons were covered with what appeared to be bicycle wheel puncture-repair patches.

Waste not, want not, was the mantra of this lady's house. And when it came to make-up, I'm not sure this lady had ever used any – her complexion was best described as 'ruddy'. She was also surrounded by a pack of dogs of all shapes and sizes, so was very keen to meet Worm. Introductions complete, we walked back into the dining room of the farmhouse.

'I'd like to put this vase into one of your sales,' she said, passing me a blue and white Chinese vase that was sitting on the dining-room table. I picked it up and looked at it; I could see that it had some age, and the quality of the painting looked very precise. Age was a tricky one with Chinese pots – as far as I could see, there was not much difference between a vase that was 500 years old and one that was 150 years old. As I stood there, it did occur to me that there wasn't much I could say in the way of advice; in my view the vase was probably eighteenth century and was probably worth between £3,000 and £5,000.

There were probably too many probablys in that.

'Philip, I've been offered five thousand pounds for the vase,' she informed me. That seemed a good offer in my limited judgement. 'But I've seen that Chinese porcelain is doing really well at auction, so I want to put it into a sale and take my chances.' I was happy with that, but did tell her that I couldn't really offer any advice.

As we chatted, she told me that the vase was bought at the turn of the nineteenth century by a relative who was a high-ranking army officer who had served in China. To enforce that, she showed me a photograph of the gent in question in full uniform standing next to a fireplace, which was interesting enough, but on the mantelpiece behind the striking military man was the vase itself. This provenance would help with the sale of the vase, and I packed it carefully into a cardboard box and took it back to the saleroom with me.

I decided to put the 'Edwardian table' and the Chinese vase into the same sale, and include an illustration of the vase in our advertising; the fact that the sale was also going to be online should ensure maximum exposure for it. Sure enough, when the sale went 'live', the vase was obviously going to be the star of the show. There was interest from mainland China, as well as one of the world's leading specialists, who telephoned to make an appointment to see it before the sale formally went on view. I met him at the saleroom and he was a delightful man. He booked a telephone line to bid on the sale day, but when I asked him what he thought it would make, I simply got a smile.

'Don't worry – it'll make what it's worth.'

There was that phrase again. The vase was clearly going to do far better than my £5,000–8,000 estimate, though at this stage I didn't have a clue what it would make and the estimate was based on the figure she had been offered for it. The main worry was that the interest from China was based solely on my description and photographs – I hoped I had got it right; if it was wrong, would the buyer pay for it? There were a number of horror stories of lots not being paid for and I was getting twitchier by the day. One particular mainland China client seemed very keen and had also booked a phone line to bid on the sale day; he was really enthusiastic after I told him about the photograph with the vase on the mantlepiece.

The little 'Edwardian table' had also generated some interest, which was good, though I was a little put out that the vendor called to say she was going to be there on the sale day. I'm not sure why, but I am always nervous when vendors tell me they are going to be at the sale to see 'how it goes' – I've never been good with an audience.

There was the usual crowd of regulars in the saleroom milling around with a hubbub of chatter, which often made me think that auctions have always been a meeting place, whether it be a cattle market or an antique sale. I scanned the assembled throng to see if I could spot any new faces that might have come for the vase, but there didn't seem to be an international man of mystery with a penchant for oriental pots in the saleroom. It looked as if the bidding would be between the two telephone bidders and whoever the internet threw up.

At that moment the main saleroom door opened. I looked up, hoping it might be a bidder for the vase. It wasn't – it was the 'Edwardian table' lady – and talk about a grand entrance. Her back-combed hair was almost as tall as she was, the shoulder pads were at a similar level to her ears, and she was wearing a fluorescent yellow suit that looked as if it had been too close to the nuclear accident at Chernobyl.

My efforts to avoid eye contact failed as she clocked me and strode over.

'I've no doubt my Edwardian table will fly, Mr Serrell,' she said in the very best pantomime stage whisper, and as she walked past, she followed it with, 'Style, Mr Serrell – don't forget style.'

Frankly, I was more concerned about the Chinese vase than any style lesson from her. My two main worries were: what if neither of the phone bidders bid, and what if the Chinese buyer bought it and didn't pay?

I got onto the rostrum and made the usual saleroom announcements before offering the first one hundred lots. If I'm honest, I probably didn't give those first lots the attention I should have done, as the 'what ifs' were starting to haunt me. The internet was active, but it wasn't exactly setting the world on fire in terms of winning, or even high underbids. Perhaps it would come alive when the vase came up – now was the time I would find out.

'Lot number 112. The Chinese vase. Bid me . . . £5,000?'

As an auctioneer, you know you have a bidder on the internet when the screen in front of you lights up – it will also tell you the country of origin of the bid. I wanted to see it flashing in front of me with the whole of mainland China bidding on it, but at the same time, when it came to payment I wanted the man who had viewed it to buy it.

I waited and waited . . . nothing.

Nervously I asked if the thing was plugged in and working properly. It was, but the screen remained blank. It was time to look around the room; perhaps the buyer would be a bidder who had crept in at the last minute. Nothing. It's a strange feeling how anticipation can turn to blind panic – all these emotions whilst trying to look as cool as a cucumber on the rostrum.

My last hope was the phones. Eventually one of them bid, which galvanised the other into activity. There may have been only two phone bidders, but they were both equally determined; on through the £20,000 barrier they went, and on. In between the two phones battling against one another, I kept glancing at the screen, which remained a blank. I didn't know who was on which phone, but I was hoping it was our preferred man.

On through £30,000 and £40,000 and only when we got to £50,000 did it slow down slightly, as the two bidders became more deliberate. Finally the gavel dropped at £58,000. I was delighted, but a little apprehensive. I hoped beyond all hope that it was the UK-based buyer and not a Chinese takeaway – selling it was one thing; getting paid for it was a different ball game altogether.

I continued with the sale, not really concentrating, as I asked Windy to find out who the buyer was. Eventually he came back – it had sold to the buyer in mainland China. Well, there was nothing I could do about it now. I had to carry on with the job in hand and concentrate on the sale. The next hundred lots or so passed without incident, until I noticed the yellow shoulder-padded apparition had reappeared in the saleroom, so I assumed we weren't too far away from her little 'Edwardian table'.

Sometimes when you are on the rostrum it's similar to an out-of-body experience; you can hear yourself talking and you are aware what is going on, yet you are totally distant from it all. I was snapped back to reality, hearing myself say, 'Lot number 237. The Chinese altar table – start me at £100?'

The room was completely unmoved by my request, almost to a point of disinterest. My lady client was staring at the saleroom audience in such a manner as to dare them not to bid. Still silence. This seemed to take an eternity, but in reality it was only a few seconds, when suddenly the computer screen in front of me lit up like the Blackpool illuminations. In fact, I couldn't keep up with it as it flashed its way to £29,000. I really hadn't seen that coming, as I had been totally preoccupied with the vase.

At the end of the auction it was a question of clearing the sale up, seeing who had bought what and how they were going to pay for it. I was in the office going through the sheets, when my style queen strode into the office.

'Style, Mr Serrell, style! I told you I had it – I think I've got an eye for antiques. I knew that little Edwardian table was a bit special.'

There seemed little or no point in telling her that it was actually a Chinese altar table and, far from being Edwardian, was more likely hundreds of years old.

'Mr Serrell, I shall be using my eye to buy more things and bring them to you to sell.' This was just what the antique world and I needed – a lucky punter who regarded themselves as an expert.

Her table had been bought by a United Kingdom-based private collector, and during a telephone conversation he told me that he intended to come to Malvern in the next seven days to collect and pay for the table. This he duly did and explained that he favoured bidding via the internet as it provided him with total anonymity. The reason it had made so much in my saleroom compared to when it was sold first time round was solely, in my view, down to the fact that our sale was online and the first wasn't.

It was time to contact the buyer of the vase; I bit the bullet and made the call. The telephone was picked up in China and I was speaking to someone with an accent that was more English than mine.

'Mr Serrell, I shall arrange to have the funds transferred to you within the next three days and will then contact you when I can come over to collect it.' I believe the expression is, 'Your cheque's in the post and I'll still love you in the morning,' but true to his word the funds were in the firm's bank account within the prescribed three days.

'Mr Serrell, I've been back to the auction I got the table from and I've bought a chair for your next sale.' It was the altar table lady and she was back with a vengeance. 'I think you'll agree this little chair has something.'

She had got Windy to carry it in for her and he was five paces behind with her latest purchase. I could scarcely believe it – he was carrying a Victorian chair that had been painted a battleship grey and upholstered in a fake zebra skin.

'I got this for eighty pounds and I think with your internet it should do really well.'

I didn't share her view, but after recent experiences I decided to keep my own counsel and included it in the next sale with an £80 reserve on it. It was not sold – in fact it went into three sales with an ever-decreasing reserve and eventually sold for £25, which in my opinion was about £24 more than it was worth. She was, however, not to be deterred in any way.

'Mr Serrell, I think my style might be more London-orientated. I hope you won't be disappointed, but I think my market place is there, rather than in the provinces.'

My loss was Sotheby's and Christie's gain.

It was now about four months since the sale and I contacted the Chinese vase buyer to ask when he intended to come and pick it up. He gave me a date and in eight weeks he arrived to pick up his pot. I hoped he was going to be happy with it – I had the money, but he needed to be satisfied with what he had bought; especially since his bid was based on my photographs and description.

He arrived at the saleroom with his wife to collect the vase; they were a delightful couple, though her command of the Queen's English was not as proficient as his. The pair of them were immaculately turned out; during our conversation, he told me they had an apartment in London where they came once a year for an extended holiday. I got the vase out for him to see.

'Mr Serrell, may I please have a word.'

This didn't sound good. I had paid out my client and if there was an issue, I could see myself holding a £58,000 problem.

'I am very pleased with the vase. My wife, however, doesn't know how much I spend on the pieces I buy for our collection. I've told her this vase was £5,800. I would be very grateful if you didn't enlighten her.' As a broad smile appeared on his face and he burst out laughing it dawned on me that this was a joke and his attempt at humour.

I was at home recounting the story to Rose and playing with Worm, when the phone rang. I've made a lifelong habit of not answering the phone and so left it to Rose; from the conversation it was obviously her mother. It never ceased to amaze me how two ladies could talk for so long about absolutely nothing and still not arrive at a conclusion.

'Daddy would like a quick word.'

Though I had been accepted into the Hall household, her father still made me very nervous; I don't know why, but I always felt as if I was being hauled before the headmaster for a good cussing. A casual chat was never an option with him; he would never use ten words when one would do.

'What did he want?' she asked when I put the phone down.

Well, in the few words he spoke to me, he told me that he had another job for me. The sheet job hadn't been the most intellectually challenging, but it had produced a healthy fee for the firm and had also kept my father away from my mother. Rose's father had given me the telephone number of another client who was in financial difficulty, and he wanted me to make an appointment to go and see if his stock was worth anything.

I wandered into the saleroom later than normal the next morning, having taken Worm for a walk first thing.

'Morning, Phil,' was a pleasant greeting from Windy. He was standing still, so that was all I got. 'Some bloke's got a watch he wants to sell – don't think it's worth much. Sounds like one of those cheap Indian things. Said it was a Philip Patel or something like that.'

I had no idea what he was talking about, but took the number and was on my way to the office when he added, 'And some other bloke called Wenlock wants you to call him. Said you'd know what it was about.'

I did indeed. Mr Wenlock owned the bureau bookcase that had got me so excited some time back. It was a case of mixed emotions for me; I was pleased that he might want to sell it and somewhat anxious that I had got the price horribly wrong.

My first phone call was to the client of Rose's father to fix an appointment for later that afternoon, which was duly made. I then called the Indian watch man – I must admit I was a bit flummoxed, as I had never heard of Philip Patel, but was prepared to learn.

'Mr Serrell, it's something of a family heirloom, but we'd like to sell it; I can bring it in at lunchtime for you to have a look at.' Well, that seemed like a good idea and gave me a couple of hours to see what I could find out about his watch. One more call to make, to Mr Wenlock.

'Ah, Mr Serrell, thank you for returning my call,' he said, in a completely flat, monotone voice; emotion and Mr Wenlock were strange bedfellows. 'We'd like to sell our piece of furniture that you saw – I think you said it should make thirty thousand pounds?'

Actually, I think I had said twenty to thirty, but as in all these cases, the lower figure is always forgotten. I arranged to go and see him.

It was time to see if I could find out more about the Indian watch. I got every watch book out of the limited saleroom library I could find, phoned up watch dealers I knew and trawled through the internet, but could find nothing at all. The watch man came in with a box about nine inches wide wrapped in brown cloth. We sat down in the office and chatted as he unwrapped his parcel and explained that his grandfather had bought the watch. It was always intended to be passed from father to son, but as he and his wife had no children, they had decided to sell it.

'It's been a very difficult decision, but it's time to part with it, I think.'

Windy was a very loyal, keen and enthusiastic saleroom porter, but there were times I could quite cheerfully have punched him. This was one of the times. Philip Patel was in fact Patek Philippe – probably one of the world's greatest watchmakers.

'It's a real wrench to sell it – I feel the wrath of my forebears might strike me down.'

I made an excuse and disappeared to the main office to look up some comparable prices on the computer. It wasn't the most desirable style of watch; not the most complicated of movements, nor in a precious metal case, but still probably worth between £2,000 and £4,000. As I walked out of the office, Windy walked in, with accompanying soundbite.

'That Indian watch any good, Phil? Probably one of those things you get in a market.'

At that point I had two urges, both of which I resisted; one was to enlighten him and the other was to throw something at him. I simply smiled and walked back to the watchman to give him the good news. The thing about good news is that it might be good in one person's eyes, but not necessarily in others. It was plainly obvious that when I imparted my thoughts on its value, he was not impressed.

'I was hoping it might make six to ten thousand. I'm not really sure we will want to sell it for that. We will have a think, but I do hope I haven't wasted your time.'

It most definitely was not a waste of time, as meeting new potential clients is always a good thing, but when he said that I knew it wouldn't be coming in for sale.

Well, not today anyway.

Chapter 9

Meet the Inventor

I set off in my car to see the client of Rose's father, who lived in one of the villages on the outskirts of Worcester. Worm came with me and was ensconced on the back seat. The address I was heading for was Glebe Barn.

I didn't think I would have too much problem finding it, as I headed down Glebe Lane, but I was wrong. At the end of the lane there were a number of properties, with the first big house proudly displaying a plaque, 'Glebe House'. I drove past it to see a converted coach house with another sign outside, 'Glebe Coach House'. I carried on, driving past 'Glebe View', 'Glebe Tallet', and on it went. I was definitely in the land of cast-iron house name plaques and 4x4 vehicles that had never seen a field.

As I drove further on, the properties became less grand, but still had the 'Glebe' connection. I had passed a church as I drove down the lane and knew that 'glebe land' was an area of land attached to a parish church. It was either owned by the church or produced an income for the church and its priest.

At the end of the lane I could see a ramshackle barn that few, if any, self-respecting cows, sheep or pigs would go inside. I parked up and knocked on the door, which was like nothing I had seen before; it appeared to be made out of wooden pallets, with homespun wrought-iron hinges that were so heavy they would have sunk the *Ark Royal*. I immediately regretted knocking on the door as I started pulling a raft of splinters from the knuckles on my right hand. I was loath to knock again, but after what seemed like an eternity with no response, I had no option but to try once more. This time I used my left hand with the same result, leaving me with two handfuls of splinters; I now had hedgehog hands.

Eventually I thought I could hear footsteps walking towards the door; though that was not exactly how they sounded. It was more akin to someone shuffling along wearing a pair of tambourines on wooden planks. The door creaked open and I was welcomed by a lady. She looked about forty-five, but could have been anywhere between thirty and sixty, and the noises I heard were explained by the wooden clogs on her feet and a bizarre arrangement of bells sewn to the hem of her cardigan.

She asked me in and as we walked down the hallway, she didn't lift her feet, but dragged them along the old boarded floor. What really stood out was the cardigan and her hair. Both were grey and long and seemed to merge into one – in fact, her cardigan could have been knitted out of her hair – and it was trimmed by a ribbon of bells that made her look like an exile from Woodstock in 1969.

'You've come to see my husband,' she said, as we continued to walk. 'He's in the barn annexe at the end of the hall.' We moved into a two-storey, floor-to-ceiling room the size of a large double garage. I had never been in such a place before. To the uneducated eye, in fact to any eye, it was full of scrap metal and junk. There were machines and contraptions straight out of a bad science fiction movie.

At the end of the room was a man in a brown smock coat, similar to the one my grandfather used to wear to milk the cows. The lady of the house introduced us. 'This is my husband,' she said and as he turned round, 'This is Mr Serrell.'

Standing in front of me was Doc Brown out of the *Back to the Future* films; except he had a slightly more crazy, vacant look about him.

'Ah, Mr Serrell. I believe Mr Hall has asked you to come and see me.'

We started to talk and he told me that he was an inventor, 'though as yet I'm probably in the prototype stage with my inventions.' He walked me over to a pile of twisted metal in the corner that was the size of a fork-lift truck .

'It's the Mark One prototype blackcurrant harvester; designed for the commercial blackcurrant farmer.'

I didn't know what to say as we both looked at what could have been a losing contender from *Robot Wars*. I asked him why it was only the Mark One prototype. 'Basically, Mr Serrell, I hadn't realised that you would need to take the machine to the bush, rather than the other way round.'

I could see that being a problem. Another design fault was that the contraption was powered by electricity; it would need an extension lead to beat them all, as well as a power point in the corner of the field. The only other option was to take the bush to the machine, and I couldn't see the blackcurrant growers of Great Britain digging up their blackcurrant plants and rushing to Glebe Barn with them.

'There is another issue, however; possibly more serious.' I couldn't see what could be more serious than inventing a machine to work in a field that you couldn't use in a field; nonetheless, I thought it was polite to ask him what that other issue was.

'The main design issue is the rotating arms that take the currants off the bush. I misjudged the spin at which they rotated – too fast. They destroyed the bush as they spun round shaking the currants off.'

So the two flaws in the invention were that you couldn't use it in a field and if you could, it destroyed the bush.

'My other invention is a device to squeeze the last bit of toothpaste out of the tube.'

I could hardly wait. I wasn't sure that this was a problem that required a remedy, but I was prepared to listen.

'Mr Serrell, like all the best inventions, mine is simple in the extreme – it relies on water pressure to squeeze the tube.'

My father always reckoned that Colman's made their money out of the mustard that was left on the side of the plate. I imagine it was the same for Mr Colgate. If it was such a good idea and was so simple, I couldn't see why it hadn't been done before.

'There's one small issue,' he said, as we walked over towards a plastic container the size of a galvanised dustbin. 'It's the volume of water required to extract that last amount from the tube. Here's the prototype.' We looked down at the plastic dustbin, which I could now see was full of water.

It was at this moment I wondered if Rose's father had a sense of humour that I hadn't yet discovered and this whole meeting was a complete wind-up. I looked at the container and worked out very roughly that the weight of water would be equivalent to my own weight.

'We had the Mark One installed in our bathroom and it worked very well, albeit there were a couple of teething problems.' I was eager to find out what they were. 'Well, the size of it meant it was very difficult to open the bathroom door,'

– I could see that being a problem – 'and the weight of it pulled the partition wall down.'

I nearly choked as I tried turning a laugh into a cough. I couldn't see what my role would actually be in helping our would-be inventor.

'Mr Hall said you might be able to help me in disposing of my two machines, or better still perhaps, come up with someone who might want to invest in the business?'

I was going to point out that I was an auctioneer not a magician; the demand for bush – and wall-destroying machines in harvesting blackcurrants and a smidgeon of toothpaste was going to be limited at best. As for finding an investor – there was more chance of an ice shortage at the South Pole.

It was time for me to make an exit and let our inventor down as gently as possible. I told him that I didn't hold out much, if any, hope at all for selling his machines, or finding anyone bonkers enough to invest money in him.

'Pity – I've got a really good idea for an automatic shoe polisher.'

At this I grabbed the front door to get out, thereby ensuring the splinters from the door were not only on my knuckles, but on the palms of my hands, too.

As it was fairly late on and I was driving over Castlemorton Common, I decided not to go back to the saleroom, but take Worm for a walk before heading home. After a good, brisk walk across the common, I had built up an appetite, and as I walked through the door the smell of whatever Rose was cooking for supper wafted through our house.

'How did you get on with Daddy's client?'

I was about to answer when the phone rang. It was her father asking for me.

The conversation was one-sided, to say the least, in that I didn't really get the chance to say anything other than yes or no. When I put the phone down, Rose asked, 'What did Daddy want?'

Put simply, Rose's father was a lovely man, but sometimes his grasp of reality was tenuous in the extreme. The inventor man was also out of the same mould; neither of them could quite understand that at best his inventions were pieces of sculpture, not very good ones at that, and at worst they looked as if they had fallen off the back of the council refuse cart.

Bless her, Rose was very much her father's daughter.

'Surely someone could do something with them? It seems such a good idea!'

I shut up as I realised that discretion was the better part of valour.

I was looking forward to seeing the Wenlocks' bureau, but at the same time I was still hesitant about my valuation; I had no idea whether I was right or wrong. Before my visit to them, however, I had a number of appointments to deal with and a fairly mundane auction in the saleroom.

The auction world is one of feast or famine and we'd had some spectacular results, but latterly things were looking a bit lean. When I left the saleroom for my first call, all I could see furniture-wise in the next auction was a stack of wardrobes – and not very good ones at that. I knew a second-hand dealer who reckoned that plywood came from the ply tree, and somebody must have cleared a whole ply forest to make these wardrobes. The problem was that most of them had more value as firewood than as antique pieces of furniture.

I have always believed that when work is quiet, the more you chase it the more it moves away from you, and part of being in business is learning the cycles of good and not so good times. I arrived at my first appointment for the day, which Windy had told me was to look at a collection of royal memorabilia. My imagination was in overdrive and I had a vision of a houseful of late seventeenth-century Delft plates and eighteenth-century fine English porcelain – all decorated with the monarchs of the day.

The house was a typical 1960s semi-detached example, where the local double-glazing salesman had done a really good job – for himself. There was not a sign of natural timber anywhere, but an array of UPVC window and door frames. As I was about to knock on the front door, I was confronted by a glass leaded-light representation of Her Majesty the Queen. At least that's who I think it was meant to be, though on close inspection it resembled a perma-tanned Bette Midler wearing a crown.

I knocked on the door using the reproduction brass door knocker in the form of a corgi; the dog that is – not a gas fitter. No response at all, so I tried again with the same result. There was a bell push set into the plastic door frame, so I gave it a press and it chimed the opening bars to God Save the Queen, but with the last three notes sounding garbled as if a battery was going flat or the clockwork mechanism needed rewinding.

It had the desired effect, because the front door opened. I know I have a trait of standing with my mouth wide open as if catching flies – this normally happens when I'm lost for words – and this was one of those moments.

Standing in front of me was a lady who had modelled herself on Dame Barbara Cartland, but she hadn't quite got it right, although they were about the same age. She wore an elaborate hat that even ladies at Ascot would be shy about wearing, especially in their own home. She offered me a white gloved hand with the line, 'Call me Elizabeth – do come in.'

I didn't know whether to curtsey. As I walked in, it was clear this lady had a complete obsession with the Queen in particular, and the Royal Family in general. There was royal clutter everywhere, but unfortunately I couldn't see anything remotely like a William III delft plate or a George III Worcester mug.

I was ushered into the sitting room and to a chair that had a huge cushion with Prince Philip's face on it. As I lowered myself with as much reverence as I could onto the royal visage, I looked around the room. The walls were covered with several homespun tapestries of the Queen in various poses and the shelves were covered with royal memorabilia of the trinket variety. The majority of it would not have looked out of place on the 'one win' prize shelf of a seafront promenade bingo hall. (With the very greatest respect to one of our great British seaside institutions.)

It was at that moment that I looked across and noticed what she was wearing on her feet: a pair of Liz and Phil *Spitting Image* puppet slippers. It was difficult to take my eyes off them and keep a straight face. This was going to need a great deal of concentration.

'Mr Serrell, I want to sell my entire collection, I think you'll agree it's very special.' There was no doubting that. 'Do you think a museum might be interested?' I'm not sure what museum she had in mind, but they would need a very good sense of humour.

'Do have a look around my collection. I'll wait here and leave you to wander; you might need some time to take it all in.'

I wandered around the house; in fact I went round it twice, it was so difficult to take everything in on a first viewing. This was going to be tricky; she was a lovely lady on the far side of eccentric, but her collection was not worth a light. It looked to me as if she had spent a king's ransom on her royal memorabilia, but her purchases had been made with the heart and not the head. In terms of investment, most of the pieces fell into the lead balloon category – there was not likely to be much demand for them.

I walked back into her sitting room, wondering how to break the bad news.

'Mr Serrell, don't worry,' she smiled, 'I know it's not worth anything. I was teasing you a little.' I was relieved that her expectations weren't that great; she went on to explain that she was moving into sheltered accommodation and it all had to go.

'The thing is, Mr Serrell, I've had so much pleasure in collecting these things. I know I'm not going to get my money back, or anything like it, but the whole process of collecting has given me so much pleasure.'

It was at that moment that it dawned on me this was true for so many collectors; it's the thrill of the chase. I've met a number of collectors through the years who, having put a collection together, then lost interest completely.

'So all I want you to do is help me clear it all and if I get anything back after I've paid the costs, I shall be delighted.' I was warming to her – realism is a great quality. I explained that Big Nige would come round and pack it all up and take it to the saleroom; I also told her that out of necessity, we would make fairly big lots of it all.

That done, it was time to apply my mind to bureau book-cases, or one in particular, as I drove to the Wenlocks' house.

'Mr Serrell, do come in. We would like to enter our bureau into one of your sales.'

Economy, in every sense, was a watchword for Mr Wenlock; he was a man who didn't give too much away. I thought the best thing I could do was get Big Nige to collect it and take it to the saleroom so, hopefully, I could find out a little more about it.

'Thank you, and if you could get back to me when you have more information to hand, I would be grateful. We will then decide what reserve to place on it before the auction.'

I had initially thought that Mr Wenlock was a cold fish, but I think I had misjudged him. He was a decent sort of chap. His nature was such that he was quiet, reserved and thorough in the way he dealt with things. At least I had a chance of discovering more about the bureau before I confirmed my estimate.

'Bloody hell, Phil – you've surpassed yourself here, mate,' was the opening remark from a dealer as I walked into the saleroom on auction day. 'You been raiding the royal skips?' came from another of the saleroom regulars.

I tried to protest my innocence, but these two could smell blood and this was too good an opportunity to waste. 'Is the Queen downsizing ... Sotheby's must be sick they missed this one,' set the tone of some good-natured humour at my expense. I decided to ignore it and made my way through the saleroom past a mountain of Charles and Diana commemorative plates and plywood wardrobes. If the room was full of anti-royalists who didn't hang up their clothes, I was in for a lean time.

'Mr Surel – could I have a word?'

It was a voice that came from behind me, was the coarse side of gravelly and was accompanied by a tap on the shoulder that would have floored lesser men. If you have a surname like mine, you have to expect to be called a variety of things; I've had Cyril, Surrelle and Surple, but this was a new one on me. I turned round to see who it was this time, and as I did so it went very dark, as if all the lights had been turned out. In front of me was an absolute ox of a man, about six feet two and weighing well over seventeen stone. He thrust a hand the size of a coal shovel at me and as we shook hands, I tried not to show any pain at his vice-like grip.

'Mr Surel – I'm interested in yer robes.'

I did think for a moment he might be referring to some ermine-trimmed cloak belonging to the royal household, but thankfully it was the myriad of plywood wardrobes that were leaning against every wall – and often one another – in the saleroom.

This chap was huge – he had on a pair of massive, steel toe-cap boots that must have been at least a size fourteen, a pair of very old-school jeans that sat below his very ample stomach and a lumberjack shirt that might have fitted him when he was twelve. The only buttons that were done up were the bottom three, exposing a remarkably hairy chest. He had Popeye-style tattoos on his arms and a huge, balding head with a five o'clock shadow like barbed-wire stubble. This was not a modern man and I can't imagine he had moisturiser on the shelf in his bathroom.

'Mr Surel, my name's Hollis, Frank Hollis, and my missus has opened a dress shop.' This was interesting, but I wasn't sure it was relevant to today's sale. 'I was thinking, Mr Surel, if folks buy dresses off 'er, they're gonna need somewhere to hang 'em.'

I couldn't fault his logic, but I did feel that most folks were going to be fully sorted when it came to hanging space. Still, I didn't want to put him off, as I had about fifteen wardrobes to sell, although it looked like more; I'm sure the things bred overnight when they were left on their own in the saleroom.

The sale started and the royal memorabilia was making not bad money; if it carried on at this rate, I could stick a 'By Royal Appointment' sign over the saleroom door. I had put the memorabilia into boxes of fairly large lots, about sixty in total, and they were selling for between £50 and £100 a go. Either the people of Malvern were a bigger bunch of royalists than I thought, or the car booters who came to the saleroom to stock up could see a bigger market than I could.

The saleroom was a forest of hands holding up bidding cards with the buyer's number on them; gone were the days of shouting out your name at an auction. Having said that, I still treasure the day I knocked a lot down to a gentleman at the front of the saleroom and asked him for his name. 'Bennett,' came the reply and as we already had one Bennett who had bought something, I asked him for his Christian name. 'Gordon Bennett!' was the response – it still brings a smile to my face.

I hadn't got to the wardrobes yet, that pleasure was about ten lots away. Coming up next were a pair of *Spitting Image* slippers. HM the Queen – the Malvern one – had told me that she bought two pairs when they came out; one pair to wear and another pair to keep as part of her collection in their original box, and these were the second pair. I was staggered when these made £65; the lady who bought them was so pleased when she walked past me, saying, 'Ooh, I'm so chuffed – I can put them next to me Lady Di and Prince Charlie ones. I only need to get me Denis and Maggie ones now.'

'Lot 97 – the 1930s wardrobe. Twenty pounds, someone?' Silence. 'Ten pounds?' Silence. 'Five someone?' More silence. 'Two anywhere – please?' This was turning into a monologue with a hint of desperation; then came salvation.

'Yes please, sir, Mr Surel – two pounds, please.' My wardrobe monologue had turned into a conversation with the big man. There was no other interest and the gavel came down. 'Hollis, Mr Surel, Frank Hollis!' he shouted out.

He was a man mountain of a bloke, but his understanding of auctions was not one of his greatest strengths. I pointed out to him that we used a number system in the saleroom these days, not a name.

'Sorry, sir, Mr Surel' – he then shouted out his phone number. This was hard work. I explained gently to him that it wasn't his telephone number I wanted, but the number they gave him when he registered to bid. 'Righto, sir, Mr Surel – I'll go and register meself now.' At that he spun around, nearly knocking over the *Spitting Image* slippers lady, and headed for the office. I carried on with the sale and a few lots later the next of the wardrobes came up.

'Where will you bid me?'

At that very moment Frank Hollis came out of the office and shouted, '104, sir, Mr Surel, 104.' I thought he was bidding at first, before I realised he was giving his buyer's number. 'Two, sir, two.' Did that mean his number was 1042, or 104 and he was bidding me £2?

'Two pounds for the 'robe, sir – two pounds for the 'robe.'

Again there was no other interest and the gavel came down. He still hadn't quite got the hang of it as he held up his bidding number card and shouted out, 'Hollis, sir, Frank Hollis.' This carried on throughout the sale and dear old Frank Hollis bought all the wardrobes for two pounds each.

'Delighted I am, sir. I reckon I'll be able to sell one to every other person that buys a dress off me missus, and I reckon I'll be able to double me money; might even be able to get a fiver for some of them.' I wasn't sure I could share his optimism.

After the sale I was outside and my new best friend was loading the first of his wardrobes into the back of his Transit van. It was almost as tight a fit as his shirt. I stood there watching as he eventually managed to get it into the van and tied the back doors together with a bungee strap. 'I'll soon have this one home and be back for the next.' I wasn't sure how the economics of this wardrobe venture were going to work, but getting his stock home was going to take him at least fifteen trips.

As the other dealers started to clear their purchases, I thought I'd ask a couple of them what they thought to the Wenlock bureau, which was stored at the back of the saleroom. The first one I showed it to looked around it; he was a good dealer in half-decent furniture and I was encouraged when he said, 'That's a good thing that, Phil; a bit beyond my normal lot, but I reckon someone in town might have a go at it.' We walked back into the saleroom and he went on, 'They might even be able to put a name to it; good luck with it – see you later, Phil.'

At that he went out to the statutory Volvo estate loaded with his new stock and drove back to his shop. The next morning I was in the saleroom when another local dealer came in to load up, and I thought there was no harm in showing the bureau to someone else.

'Don't like it, Phil; the drawers don't look right to me with that brass inlay. I wouldn't want to give big money for it.'

I wished I hadn't asked him.

Chapter 10

The Wenlock Bureau

On Monday, I went into the office and got the message everyone dreaded. 'Mr Rayer wants to see you.' He was now into his eighties and had been so kind and generous with his time towards me, I felt guilty when I didn't extend to him the same courtesy. 'He wants you to pick him up from his home at eight o'clock in the morning to go and see old Oakman, a farmer from Bromyard.'

Mr Rayer lived in a large nineteenth-century house with outbuildings and about six acres of land. Nothing too unusual about that, except it was pretty much in the middle of the city of Worcester. His wife had died some years back and he lived there on his own. It was a house I loved, not for its size and acreage, but because it was like going back in time. The house had been in the family for generations, as had most of the contents, and off the hallway was an office that epitomised him.

It was not a grand affair, but I doubt it had changed since the 1860s and if it had, the filing system certainly hadn't. There were papers and files everywhere, with several 'Rayer pipes' lying around; a bookcase full of woefully out-of-date reference books, and bits and bobs that told the story of the Rayer family for three or four generations. Everything centred on a Georgian mahogany partners desk, with a leather and mahogany armchair of similar age behind it and a patched leather armchair to the side.

It was undoubtedly a man's office, but the main attraction for me was that it had a fireplace that gave out a very comforting warmth. This was a bonus, as Mr Rayer didn't do central heating, in fact I'm not even sure he knew of its existence. This was one of those houses where you got up in the morning and the frost was on the inside of the windows rather than the outside. The SAS could have done their Arctic training in the Rayer family home.

I arrived at eight o'clock as instructed; the grass was white with frost and Mr Rayer had left his car where he usually parked it – on the lawn by the front door of the house. Settlebanks, the Rayer family home, had a number of outbuildings but no garage for the car, which always struck me as strange. I suppose it was built well before the motor car had been invented and the Rayer family had spent little on the house since then.

The windows of the house were frozen over with no sign of life, or heat, coming from within. I knocked on the front door and waited; Mr Rayer with his tin leg would take an age getting to it. No response, so I knocked again – still nothing. I wandered around the outside of the house to see if I could find any sign of life anywhere. Yet again nothing and I was beginning to get worried; I had visions of my old boss collapsed in a heap on the floor.

My next plan of action was to break a window and get into the house; I was in complete panic mode. This was a Rayer property, so I knew there would be something lying around somewhere that I could use to break in. I walked past the car and – I'm not sure why – I peered through the frosted windows. There was my old boss slumped over the steering wheel; he must have been there all night, as there were no fresh tyre tracks through the frost on the lawn.

I was in a real state; he was an old man and there was no way he could have survived a night outside without suffering hypothermia. I would have to break into the car. Whilst I was working out what to do, I was also trying to figure out what I should say to his three children; I had never had to break news like this before. I peered into the car again and the body was still motionless inside. I imagined he had fallen asleep and not woken up; his body collapsing over the steering wheel.

I tried the handle and surprisingly the door was not locked. I opened it and couldn't mistake the heavy snoring that came from within and it occurred to me that corpses aren't meant to snore. I shook him really hard – as much out of relief as anything else.

'You want to be careful waking someone like that, Philip. You could give someone a heart attack!'

I could have hugged him; apparently he had been out to a meeting, got back late and then fell asleep in the car. I suppose the sub-zero temperatures in his house had prepared him for such an eventuality.

'You'd better drive, Philip.'

This was almost unheard of – he was a stubbornly independent man and having someone drive him around was not on his agenda. It had been noticeable that he was slowing down a bit and it was probably time for him to consider retirement. Sooner or later someone would need to have a word with him and I was pretty sure that it would have to be me.

The Oakman family lived on a smallholding just outside Bromyard. I was always amused that Mr Rayer referred to him as 'Old Oakman', when he was about five years younger than my one-legged boss. (It was odd, because technically I was *his* boss, as he was now a consultant to the firm, but to me he was always the boss. It wasn't until two years after he died that I felt able to refer to him as Ted.)

We went into the Oakman kitchen, where the old AGA was pumping out some very welcome heat.

'Would you like a drink?'

To most folk this would have meant tea or coffee, but Harold Oakman was from an older generation and a visit from Mr Rayer meant the scotch bottle came out. I was hugely relieved that I was driving when I saw the measures that were poured. I was nothing more than Mr Rayer's chauffeur on a trip like this, but it was lovely to sit back and listen to these two talk and reminisce about the old days.

'Ted, thank you for coming out to see me. None of us are getting any younger and I think it's time for me to pack up.'

Mr Rayer replied, 'Harold, if the time is right, you'll know.'

The gist of our trip was that there was nothing Mr Oakman wanted us to do professionally; he simply wanted to let Mr Rayer know he was going to retire. I don't know why, but I felt sad; these two had known one another for the thick end of fifty years. He told us that his son was going to continue with the farm, and that he and his wife were going to have a bungalow built in one of the fields, where they would live. There was an obvious bond between the two of them and it was lovely to witness it.

We got back in the car and set off to Worcester; normally Mr Rayer would have chatted all the way back, telling me who lived at the various farms we passed and what jobs he had done, but on this trip he was unusually quiet – almost reflective. We pulled up at his house, having not spoken a word on the trip back.

'Philip, I think my time has come to call it a day, too. You'd better ask Nigel to come and clear my office.'

He was referring to his room in the firm's Worcester office, rather than his home. I was sorry to hear this, but almost relieved too, as it would have been awful for me to have made the decision for him. I called Big Nige, whose reaction was, 'Gum – crikey,' and made the arrangements for us to clear his office.

It was a testament to Mr Rayer that his office in Worcester was on the first floor and he refused to move to the ground floor, as it would mean he was getting special attention. Ordinarily I would have been delighted to take his furniture for sale at auction, as it was a mixture from the late Georgian and early Victorian eras, but this was a really sad day for me. I suspect I was more upset than he was, because I owed him so much. He had a good writing table, office chair, side table, bookcase and a secretaire bookcase that would all sell well. Mr Rayer sat in his chair directing operations, as Big Nige removed things to his van outside.

All of the furniture had to go, but the smaller items such as his books were divided into two piles – one for the saleroom and one for his office at home. Thankfully, Mr Rayer decided to take most of the books home, as I didn't think there would be much demand for *Theory and Practical Auction Law 1907*. Slowly we cleared the office around him until it was only him left sitting on a chair and everything else had been taken to the van. I'm not ashamed to admit that there was a tear in my eye as I looked at him in the middle of an empty office.

Big Nige was the man for the moment. 'Come on, Guvnor – you'd better get up and let me take the chair, or else we'll have you in the back of the van as well.'

As soon as Mr Rayer got up, Big Nige whipped the chair out from underneath him; there was no going back. It was a sad day and the end of an era.

The good news was that all of Mr Rayer's furniture sold well and made strong money. There were two reasons for this – firstly, it was good quality furniture that was in good demand at the moment, and secondly, because it was in totally untouched condition. This was likely more by accident than design.

As I walked through to the storeroom at the back of the saleroom, Mr Wenlock's bureau bookcase caught my eye again; sooner or later I had to do something with it. It was clear to me that there was divided opinion about the bureau, particularly in terms of value. I arrived at the decision that it was time for the market to decide and the way to do that was to put it to auction.

Sir Anthony Borrington, Bt., was a lovely man who lived in Borrington Hall on the banks of the River Wye in Herefordshire. I had first met him a couple of years earlier when his uncle, Sir Ralph, had died aged eighty-two and I was called in to prepare a valuation for inheritance tax purposes.

Tony Borrington lived with his wife Sarah and two boys aged fourteen and sixteen in a modest house in Putney. He had a quietly successful job with a smallish company as an advertising executive to the media world. Sarah was a medical secretary at one of the London hospitals; both worked hard and were able to educate the boys privately and take two good holidays each year. Everything was rosy in their world until Tony had a telephone call telling him that his uncle had died. He was now Sir Anthony Borrington and he had inherited the Hall and the estate around it.

At first this sounds fantastic, but not a penny had been spent on Borrington Hall since shortly after the Second World War. There was more wiring in the place than in a transatlantic telephone cable and enough lead on the roof to cover a football pitch, so these were not going to be petty cash jobs. Added to this, there was a decorating project that made painting the Forth Bridge look like a walk in the park.

However, this paled into insignificance compared to the major problem with the Hall. Sir Ralph was a man who kept a firm eye on his wallet and his choice of land agent reflected this. The Hall was a monster of a place, and Sir Ralph and his wife had no children, so they decided to move into an estate house in the village and find someone to look after the house and land. The agent he appointed was best described as an enthusiastic amateur, rather than a professional man.

To this end, he concluded that the best way to occupy the house was to erect stud partition walls, split the house into two, and let it to two local families. The land, about a thousand acres, was let to a local farmer who was an expert at growing thistles and not much else. The real mistake was that the various tenants he created were paying only peppercorn rents, but they also had security of tenure, which meant that when Tony Borrington inherited the hall and the estate, he inherited the tenants, too.

On his uncle's death, he had two options; the first was to sell the whole lot, put some money in the bank and carry on living his comfortable Putney lifestyle – or uproot his family and move to the wastelands of Herefordshire. Tony recognised that his family had been in the house since about 1450, and felt that he had a certain responsibility to the village and the families that had relied on the estate through the years. In his eyes, the decision was simple – he had to take on the estate; so he and Sarah gave up their jobs and upped sticks to the Wye Valley to sort out a complete bugger's muddle.

Sir Ralph may not have been the most astute when it came to his professional advisers; however, Tony did tell me one lovely story about his octogenarian uncle. Apparently on the first Tuesday of every month, Sir Ralph used to catch the train from Hereford to London Paddington mid-morning, in order to be in London for a meeting from lunchtime until late afternoon. This was as regular as clockwork, every first Tuesday, for about ten years.

It wasn't until after his death that Tony discovered the family didn't have any professional advisers in London. It turned out that Sir Ralph had been going to see a lady from the W1 region of London, who would indeed have been professional, but probably not in a way that Lady Borrington might have appreciated.

Tony had become a friend, and he called me one day on his mobile phone to ask me if I would pop over to prepare an insurance valuation of a painting of one of his ancestors. The reception in this part of Herefordshire was not that good, but from what I could make out, it was of some general from the nineteenth century who had been shot. This didn't strike me as a particularly rare occurrence and, unless the general had gone on to win a Victoria Cross or something, I couldn't see it being worth a lot of money. It was interesting that he was wounded in action and this might have some impact on its value, but I was well aware of the old adage that portraits of pretty girls are worth more than crusty old generals.

I made the appointment to drive out to see Tony; it was a trip I was looking forward to as he was excellent company, the countryside was beautiful and the house, for all its faults, was stunning. I drove through the old wrought-iron entrance gates that looked so much better for not being 'straight out of the box', but showing about 150 years of wear and abuse. The drive to the house was about a mile long through a parkland of wonderful old trees; the road surface had also not benefited from any expenditure in recent years and would have proved ideal for test driving Land Rovers.

I pulled up at the house and Tony and I exchanged pleasantries as we walked into the kitchen for a coffee. No instant stuff for the Borringtons – a proper machine that provided a mainline caffeine boost.

'This place is a money pit, Philip,' he said, 'and to patch even part of the roof over the west gable is going to make a hole in fifteen thousand. There's just no end to it.'

Whilst it was hard work making ends meet, you could see that Tony was determined to keep it all together and not leave the next generation with the same issues. I reminded him that I was there to look at the portrait for insurance. He told me it was at the other end of the house, which in a three-bed semi was ten or fifteen seconds away, but here it was a fair old walk and we chatted along the way. I was keen to know more about the general, in terms of his military history campaigns and the like.

'I don't think he did anything really; if he wasn't a relative, I probably wouldn't bother with restoring it.' I was keen to know how he had been wounded. 'Shot in the eye – airgun pellet, clean as a whistle. Another on the nose and one on the ear.'

I couldn't recall a conflict in the nineteenth century that used airguns.

'Sorry, Philip, I didn't make myself clear – the boys shot him. Bit of target practice at the end of the long gallery.'

It transpired that Tony's two boys had decided to hone their airgun skills by taking pot shots at the general down the long gallery. 'I thought it would be quite fun and a bit of a talking point at dinner parties if I stuck sticking plasters over his wounds, but Sarah wouldn't hear of it. I just need a figure so I can claim on the insurance – though the claim form will make interesting reading!'

That would not be too difficult a figure to come up with; it wasn't the best painting in the world and no one of any great importance. Tony and I talked some more as we walked back through the Great Hall.

'The boys are a bit high spirited and it's probably much tougher for them than Sarah and me since we moved back from London. I actually caught them playing football in here last night.'

I shared with him one of my father's old expressions, which I thought apt. 'My old man always said you can't breed tame rabbits from wild ones!'

As we reached the far side of the Great Hall, he continued, 'They were using a tea caddy off the side table and Granny's old sewing box as goal posts. Little beggars.'

I looked down and my eyes nearly popped out. The tea caddy was a mundane nineteenth-century mahogany, two-division example that with a good following wind would have made £40. The sewing box was the most glorious stumpwork casket dating to around 1670.

Stumpwork was a form of embroidery that was practised by children of wealthy folk in the late seventeenth century. It wasn't simple embroidery, however, it was padded and raised in relief showing figures in landscapes with animals. When originally made, these things were of the most vivid colours and in fine condition. The ravages of time meant that the colours in most of them had faded horribly and the padding and stitching had deteriorated.

I asked Tony if I could have a closer look at it. 'Of course – it's normally kept in that glass box over there,' he said, pointing to a rectangular case on top of the piano, 'but at least they took it out of that before they started kicking a ball around.'

It was as good as new and the colours were fantastic; it wasn't really a box, but more of a casket. The lid opened on the top and two small doors opened at the front to reveal a mirror and a fitted interior. The condition was stunning, with no torn fabric or fading; it was breathtaking and it was hard to believe it was as old as it was.

'Sooner or later it'll get damaged here with those two. Is it worth anything?'

Does a fish swim? With caskets similar to this, there were three important issues – that's the condition, condition and condition, and this ticked the box on all three counts. I told Tony I thought it might make £10,000–15,000.

'That's a lot of money for a goal post and it might help sort the hole in the roof. If you really think you can get that for it, you'd better take it and sell it.' And that's the thing about being a country auctioneer – you never know what you're going to see next; you can go to value a painting and come back with a 300-year-old box in the back of the car.

On the way back to the saleroom, I decided to put the Wenlock lot into the same sale with a fixed reserve on it, provided Mr Wenlock was happy with that.

I was lucky to have two youngsters now working with me in the saleroom – Sophie Jones, who had first come to the saleroom on work experience some years ago, and Charles John Edward Rambridge, or Rambo. Sophie had qualified as a fine art auctioneer and Rambo was ex-public school, ex-university educated and currently studying at the Farmer

Arms, Birtsmorton. Rambo had a very clipped, upper-crust voice that made Hugh Grant sound like Danny Dyer.

They were both a calming influence on me. Sophie's view on most things was, 'It will be fine – it'll make what it'll make,' whilst Rambo was more, 'Well, er . . . I'm sure it will all, er . . . be fine.' Rambo went on holiday listening to P.G. Wodehouse on his eight-track stereo – that was the measure of the man. Windy referred to the pair of them as 'The Kids'.

I called Mr Wenlock and told him what I thought.

'Mr Serrell, we did take a second opinion and I think we would be happy if we put a reserve of thirty thousand pounds on it.' It had taken time, but it would be interesting to see what the bureau made at the auction – if indeed it sold.

The view day for the auction was really centred on two lots, Sir Anthony's casket and the Wenlock bureau, and both produced wildly differing reactions. Without exception, everyone who picked up the casket was impressed by its condition; so much so that there were already a number of telephone lines booked for bidders that couldn't make it to the auction, but wanted to bid at the sale. One of these was a lovely couple who lived about three miles from Borrington Hall; they told me that their passion was the seventeenth century and their home was furnished to reflect this.

The bureau bookcase produced a far different reaction. For every person who looked at it and thought it was wonderful, there was another who simply dismissed it as being 'not for them'. These differences of opinion are what makes the antiques trade. I was given a little heart when a dealer of some repute spent about an hour looking at the bureau and then asked me to book a telephone line.

At least that gave me some confidence, though it was shot down half an hour later when another dealer whom I respected also spent some time going through it. 'I'm just not sure – I'm going to think about it; I'm not sure if it's a marriage.' A marriage is when two pieces of furniture have been put together to give the impression that is how they started out in the world; in this instance, a low floor-standing bookcase has been put on a bureau. I had one other person who had booked a phone line, though I had no idea who he was, and I was left wondering if it was going to sell.

I was probably on my third lap of the saleroom when another top dealer walked in. I watched him take every drawer out and study each one in some detail; after a time, he walked out towards the door of the saleroom. 'Interesting piece, that,' was a cursory observation that told me nothing at all. I was more than confident the stumpwork casket would sell, but was left guessing what would happen to the bureau. It was now a matter of waiting for the auction.

Sale days are always hectic and this was no different to any other. 'Phil, some bloke wants to talk to you about a phone bid on that old desk thing.' I could always rely on Windy to bring a semblance of Worcestershire reality to the situation. It was encouraging that someone else wanted a phone line, or so I thought. However, that wasn't the case; the good dealer who had booked a line earlier was ringing up to say he wanted to cancel it. I asked him if he was coming to the auction instead and simply got, 'Sorry, Philip, change of heart. I just don't think it's for me.' So that left one phone line bidder whose identity I didn't even know – it could be someone who simply wanted to listen to my voice over the phone.

As I walked out of the office, I noticed another dealer who had come into the saleroom. He had a dealer with him whom I didn't recognise, but they walked over to me. 'Morning, Philip, we're going to have a look at your bureau. Could we take it outside into daylight, please?' I asked Windy to help them take it outside and watched as they pretty much dismantled both pieces and turned them upside down and inside out.

Rambo and Sophie took the early part of the sale and when Sir Anthony's casket came up, Rambo was on the rostrum. I took a huge amount of pleasure watching the pair of them sell and was proud when they were both acknowledged as two first-class auctioneers. I could feel myself morphing into Mr Rayer.

The casket was fairly predictable in that we knew it was a good thing, so it was no great surprise when Rambo sold it to the delighted couple of collectors who were bidding on one of the telephones; it made £19,000, which in my view showed a £5,000 premium for its exceptional condition. Where we would end up with the bureau was more in the lap of the gods, and I was in charge of the gavel when it came up.

I was on the rostrum beforehand scanning the saleroom for potential bidders. I knew I had the one telephone bidder, but the dealers who had viewed it yesterday were nowhere to be seen, and the guys who had driven up from London seemed to be wandering around the saleroom looking at other furniture in a fairly disinterested way. My main concern was that no one would hear the nerves in my voice as we came to it.

'Next, this good eighteenth-century mahogany bureau bookcase. Where do you want to start me – £30,000?' That was followed by the customary silence. I could feel myself dying on my feet as everyone in the room seemed to stare at their boots. I kept reducing my opening bid, till someone in the room shouted, 'Five thousand pounds, sir!'

I could feel my voice faltering as I started the bidding. I searched the room anxiously looking for the next bid.

Eventually the one solitary phone bidder joined in and I looked back at the guy who made the first bid, but he was a one-bid wonder and he turned away and said nothing. Then someone who I hadn't seen before, either in the saleroom or viewing, put his hand up to bid in an almost indifferent way, as if he didn't mind whether he got it or not. And that was the way it continued between him and the phone bidder – on and on and on until I could hear myself saying, 'All done and sold then,' and brought the gavel down. It had made £46,000 and sold to the telephone bidder.

When I had finished, I got off the rostrum and walked to the office. The extremes of response were bizarre: 'You swum the channel with that, Phil', 'Made the right sort of money, that did', and 'Can't see you getting paid for that!' were a selection of the remarks that came my way. It didn't finish there, as during the next week I was told I wouldn't get paid, and that it would have made only five grand in town.

That was another thing about the antiques world – never let the truth get in the way of a good story. Everybody was an expert after a lot had been sold, but nobody ventured an opinion beforehand. Well, I got paid for it pretty much straight away, it was collected and I believe the new owner was pleased with it. Mr Wenlock called me to say how delighted he was with the sale and thought we had done a good job; it's always rewarding to get that type of feedback.

One thing the whole episode taught me was that you should always back your own judgement. Sophie in the office said, 'I told you it would do alright – stuff always makes what it makes.'

Rambo added with a smile, 'I thought the casket did really well too. It's all about the auctioneer, you know.'

Chapter 11

~

The Art Deco Lady

This was followed by a relatively quiet period in the sale-room, though Sophie and Rambo were very excited by a lady who called in with an Art Deco figure to sell made out of ivory, bronze and marble. They were keen because these 1920s figures can make a lot of money, and were anxious that I call the lady straight away.

I didn't want to dampen their enthusiasm, but I was fully aware that Art Deco figures were often faked and this was likely to be one of them. I could forgive them as it was one of those things that comes with experience, and lately I had seen a number of these little figures, but nonetheless I made an appointment to go and see her; as much for them, as for the client concerned. She sounded like a delightful lady, who lived in a farmhouse to the south of Cheltenham, and I arranged to meet her in a couple of weeks' time, as she was due to go away on holiday in the meantime.

''Ere, Phil, it's time for the A team to look at a job.'

The A team that Windy was referring to was Mr Rayer, Windy and myself. This was his response to hearing my conversation with Sophie and Rambo about the Art Deco figure.

Windy and I had worked together for years now, but his ability to trump at every step continued to amaze me. He was the only man I knew who could emit the 'Trumpet Voluntary' from his behind, but only when he moved; when he stood still, silence reigned supreme.

'The Guvnor wants you, me and 'im to go and look at some proper stuff.' I could hardly wait – this was a trip out for the three of us to visit an old client of Mr Rayer's. It would be at least half a day out of my life that I would never get back. 'And 'e wants me to go specially, as I knows 'em.' That wasn't quite the gold standard of approval that I was hoping for.

We were due to meet Mr Rayer at his house the next day, which was bad news as he would insist on driving, and I had no control over when we'd get back. Mr Rayer was now only a part-time consultant, but he was still very keen to be involved with the firm.

I picked Windy up from his home. Although I had worked with him for so long, I had never met Windy's wife and I always wondered how she coped with his little problem – of which, as ever, he was blissfully unaware. Mr and Mrs Windy lived in a Victorian terraced house in Worcester and I pulled up and knocked on the front door. I didn't know whether his problem was dietary or not, but whatever he had eaten the night before was having a profound effect. I could hear him from outside the front door.

'Come on in, Phil – you 'aven't met the Missus, 'ave you?' As we walked along the hall corridor toward the room at the end, Windy backfired with every pace.

We entered the room and there was a lady sitting at a table with her back to us. I said 'Good morning' to her, but was completely ignored.

''Er's a bit Mutt and Jeff,' was Windy's explanation, so I bellowed at her and still got no recognition. 'We'll leave 'er

Phil,' said Windy, as we turned to walk out. 'I can 'ardly make meself 'erd to 'er sometimes.'

Really, I thought, well that explained a lot.

We arrived at Mr Rayer's house at 9 a.m. for a 10 a.m. appointment that was forty-five minutes' drive away, so allowing for any calamities that could befall us, it should give us plenty of time. We knocked on the front door and let ourselves in. Mr Rayer was standing in the hall, stick in hand, shouting at his dog, 'Give it back!' Turning to us, he complained, 'The bloody dog's run off with my valuation book.' Pantomime season had come early to Worcester this year.

Mr Rayer's valuation books were the size of a packet of cigarettes and he never went anywhere without them – certainly not a valuation. Somewhere in the house or garden was a yellow Labrador dog running around with Mr Rayer's notebook in his mouth. I won't go into all of the details, but it took Windy and me about twenty minutes to capture the dog and retrieve the book before we could set off. I don't know why we had to find it before we could leave, but it wasn't something I was going to question with Mr Rayer.

As we were walking towards my car, he suddenly changed course and said, 'I'll drive, Philip.'

This was going to be one of those days; I made my way to Thunderbird 4 like a condemned man. Mr Rayer was independent in the extreme, though stubborn was another word that could be used. Windy and I were both aware that you did not offer help to him at any time. We watched as he made his way to the car, stick in one hand and briefcase in the other; every step must have been painful for him. We got into the car and waited for him to struggle his way into the driver's seat.

The automatic gearbox on his car had a mind of its own; engaging a gear was a signal of intent, rather than a sign that anything was going to happen. He moved the gear lever to D for drive and we all waited; there was a lot of noise and eventually there was a bang as everything dropped into place and we lurched forward.

I was in the front seat, with Windy in the back, as we set off through Worcester. We didn't so much drive as meander, drifting from one side of the road to the other, terrifying oncoming drivers and on one occasion a pedestrian on the far pavement as we veered towards them. Mr Rayer was blissfully unaware of the mayhem. His family had been in Worcester for generations, and while he scattered all and sundry, he pointed out to us who had lived where and what they did.

I began to panic, as I could see roadworks ahead and a workman operating a Stop and Go sign, which was currently in the Stop position for traffic in our direction. I don't know if Mr Rayer intentionally drove through it, but that is exactly what he did. The look on the workmen's faces was priceless as I practised my most apologetic look, but after we passed through the roadworks, I noticed a parked police car that had witnessed the whole event. I tried to climb into the glove compartment as the police car, complete with siren and flashing lights, came chasing up behind us. It overtook us and pulled us over.

'Bloody sauce,' was Mr Rayer's view on all this. It was an expression I had heard him use many times, almost exclusively from the driver's seat. I was wondering how I would explain to his family that he had been locked up, as the policeman got out and walked to the driver's door of Thunderbird 4.

'Sorry, Mr Rayer,' he said, 'I didn't realise it was you. Drive safely now,' and with that we drove off. I'm still not sure how he got away with it.

I had no idea where we were going and who we were going to see. Life as ever with him was a voyage of discovery, but at last the information was forthcoming. 'We're going to see Old Mother Gubbins.' Well, that sorted that one out. 'She says she's got some kitchenalia she wants to sell – whatever that is.' I was now in information overload. I had learned not to ask Mr Rayer too many questions – the answers sometimes muddied the water.

Windy was sitting in the back of the car enjoying the view; whilst being in the front seat, I was close to any potential 'action' that we might have with Mr Rayer's driving. There was nothing to report as we left the city boundary and I started to relax. As we headed out towards Bromyard, we turned right in Whitbourne. This was dangerous country, as I had travelled this way before and the roads were narrow with a number of blind bends. I was well aware of this, but Mr Rayer seemed blissfully ignorant of the impending peril.

I was a nervous passenger with him at the best of times, but this intensified as Mr Rayer decided it was time to light his pipe. This was a performance when he was sitting behind a stationary desk – behind the wheel of a car, it had the potential to be horrible. He packed the bowl of his pipe and pulled a lighter from his pocket; it was more of a blow torch as it flared up like a Bunsen burner. As his cheeks puffed to get the pipe going, this was normally the most dangerous time; he was so engrossed in the process that he was unaware of anything else on the road.

Surprisingly, at this stage we weren't deviating from the road at all; it was almost as if he had a sixth sense as to where the road was – but as the pipe got going, the inside of the car filled up with smoke. The fact that he could barely see the windscreen was probably the reason Mr Rayer didn't notice the Post Office van coming straight at us.

It was like a game of chicken, where two cars hurtle toward one another at breakneck speed, neither wanting to be the first to brake or swerve out of the way. Mr Rayer wasn't going to give way – principally because he couldn't see the van coming towards us. At the last minute, the poor postie steered wildly into a gateway and, as we drove past, I could see him stopped in the middle of a farmer's sugar beet field. Mr Rayer had no idea, of course, that any of this had occurred.

After a few more miles, the smoke had cleared and I could see we were turning onto a long lane towards a farmhouse in the distance. It wasn't a question of the lane having potholes, more like the potholes had a lane. As we got closer to Old Mother Gubbins' farmhouse, I could tell this was a typical Mr Rayer job. It was a 200-year-old building that in estate agency terms was ripe for modernisation – very ripe. The one glimmer of hope was that properties like this normally housed some good old antiques that had been there since the year dot.

We knocked on the door and 'OMG' appeared. She was about seventy and her face was the colour and complexion of a house brick. 'So you're the young feller who likes kitchenalia?' she said. I admitted it was an interest – it's always been the social history of items that has appealed to me, and old kitchen utensils help tell the story of how we have lived our lives.

As we walked into the house, the furniture was typical of an old-fashioned farmhouse. I was quite looking forward to seeing her kitchenalia and not sure what to expect; anything from Victorian copper jelly moulds to treen biscuit moulds and wonderful old butter makers – I was ever hopeful. We walked into what OMG called the dairy and she pointed to a box on the floor and said, 'There you are then.'

I wasn't sure how to react, but Windy's 'bloody 'ell!' summed up the situation best. The four of us were standing looking at a box of Kilner jars; glass jars with rusty tin covers and perished rubber seals of the sort my mother used for bottled fruit. I didn't know what to say, but thankfully Mr Rayer stepped in to save me. 'We can put those in one of our sales – but they won't make you a fortune.' That was an understatement.

'Well, I just want to get rid of them,' she replied. 'I could do with the space. I was going to throw them out.'

'Mr Williams will put them in the back of the car for you.' Windy and I looked at one another before realising that Mr Rayer was talking about him; I had never heard him called Mr Williams before.

With our booty secured in the boot of the car, we made our way back to the saleroom. I was secretly hoping that another car might hit us from behind, as it was the only way I could ever see of us getting rid of the damn things.

'Philip, you had better put a reserve on the jars of twenty pounds,' he said, and before I could object, 'and you can leave a bid on for me of twenty-five pounds. I like a bit of bottled fruit.'

That was probably a measure of the man. The chances of him bottling his own fruit were remote to nil, but it was obvious that he didn't want his client to get nothing. My worry was that she might feel they had sold well and bring me some more in.

I had made the appointment to see the Art Deco figure lady and, as Sophie and Rambo were at a loose end, I thought it would be good experience for them if they came with me and met the client. We drove south of Cheltenham to a pretty Cotswold village and pulled up at a drive with a cattle grid before a sweeping entrance to a Georgian Cotswold stone house. To the right of the drive was a large pond, with examples of most native British ducks on it. Their presence was most likely due to a woman who looked to be in her seventies, and I presumed was the lady of the house, feeding them copious amounts of corn from a bucket.

'I doubt any of those would ever get airborne, looking at the corn they're eating,' piped up Sophie from the back of the car. I've never seen anyone feed ducks in a twin-set with pearls, tweed skirt and a pair of sensible brogues; she reminded me of the actress Margaret Rutherford in the old Miss Marple films.

As Rambo wound down the window, we were greeted with, 'Good morning, dear. Have you come to look at my figure?' and immediately after, 'I say – sorry, that didn't come out quite right!'

'Rather,' was Rambo's response.

'Drive up to the house and I'll meet you there.'

The gravelled drive was about one hundred yards long, with a well-manicured grass verge to either side. The driveway up to the house had a turning circle around an island with a large stone cider press in the middle of it. The lawns to the house were equally well tended and looked after, with a ha-ha at the far end – a recessed wall or barrier that doesn't interrupt the overall view; a bit like an infinity swimming pool. The house was a very impressive building too, with a series of yew trees to the right-hand side clipped to perfection in a row of peacocks.

'Rather like a visit to a stately home this, Philip.'

I was pleased I had brought Rambo and Sophie with me.

They were the next generation of the business, and it was useful for them to meet clients and to foster relationships. Mr Rayer had been so good to me in that respect; in his world there was no such thing as ownership of a client.

'I'm Mrs Cotswolds' – I've changed her name to protect her anonymity – 'I'm so pleased you were able to come and so pleased you've brought your son and daughter with you.' This may have been hugely amusing for Sophie and Rambo, but I did not see the funny side and quickly pointed out that we were work colleagues.

'I am so dreadfully sorry – gosh!' Rambo was loving this.

'Don't worry,' I said, 'it's an easy mistake to make.'

'Well, dear, you all look so young.'

Mrs Cotswolds might have dug herself out of a hole with that remark until Sophie whispered to me, 'She doesn't mean you.'

'Let me show you the figure, dear.'

I stood in the hall and looked around; it was a room with a floor area bigger than some houses and went from the ground floor, through the first floor, and up to a roof light in the ceiling. At the far end of the hall was a very imposing staircase that wound around the two side and end walls. It was very much a country-house staircase that would accommodate three or four people walking side by side up it at the same time.

There were recessed alcoves in the walls going up the staircase that housed all sorts of porcelain and other objects. The furniture in the hall was top quality and there were fine antiques and paintings, Chinese and other porcelain. There were lovely objects everywhere – I felt as if we should be paying Mrs Cotswolds an admission fee.

'Come along in, dears; I'll make us some tea in a moment.' We walked through the hall towards the staircase. 'The figure is in that second alcove on the staircase.' I looked up at the alcove in question – we were going to need either a cherry picker or a scaffold tower to get it down; a thought that was vocalised by my two 'offspring'.

'I think we're going to need a ladder,' was Sophie's suggestion, whilst Rambo came out with his customary, 'Rather'.

Mrs Cotswolds led us into the kitchen and out of a door at the rear of the house, saying, 'Follow me, dears.' We made our way to an outbuilding that, like everything else, was meticulously laid out with everything in its place. Rambo picked up a ladder that appeared to be of the right size and we made our way back into the house.

'You go and get it down, dears, and I'll make the tea and get some cake ready.'

Rambo with the ladder in the hall sounds like a suspect and a weapon in a game of *Cluedo*. It looked suspiciously as if it might come true – the way he was performing with the ladder, there was every chance I would kill him.

Sophie shouted, 'Look out, Rambo!', which was probably not a good thing to do. Instead of holding the ladder upright, he was carrying it parallel to the floor, so when she shouted his immediate reaction was to turn around. It was like a classic farce; as he spun round, the end of the ladder caught a vase of flowers, knocking them off the table they were sitting on. It was one of those moments – I could see it tumbling to the floor in slow motion, but there was nothing I could do about it.

Mrs Cotswolds came in just as it smashed to pieces on the floor. I looked at Sophie and she looked at me. Rambo simply stood there and was about to mutter something when she said, 'Don't worry, dear. It was a modern thing that a friend gave me last Christmas.' That was a good job, because it was now in a hundred pieces lying on the floor.

'I am most awfully sorry,' mumbled Rambo, and as he bent down he nearly took out a watercolour on the far wall with the ladder he was still holding.

'Charles, for God's sake hold the bloody thing upright!' As ever, Sophie put a practical take on the situation and Rambo stood bolt upright, grasping the ladder firmly to his side like a sentry on duty outside Buckingham Palace; at least in this position he was unlikely to knock anything else over.

'Have your tea and cake, dears, before you get it down.'

Sophie and I watched as Rambo stood completely still, whilst holding on to the ladder and balancing a plate with a piece of Madeira cake on it and a cup of tea on its saucer; Mrs Cotswolds didn't do mugs. I've seen guys at the circus spinning plates on sticks and struggling to keep them all airborne; this was what Rambo was doing, except he was trying to drink his tea and eat his cake at the same time.

'I'll leave you to it, dears, and call me when you've done.'

At this stage, as the figure was about eighteen feet up in the air, I still wasn't sure whether it was a reproduction or not; though having been in the house and seen the other contents, I did think that it was unlikely.

'While you're doing that, dear, somewhere I've got a photograph of it when my parents lived at the big house. It's black and white and a bit grainy.' That would definitely indicate that it was not repro; I also wondered how large the big house was, if it was bigger than the house we were in now.

Rambo was balancing the ladder up against the wall of the hall. He had gone from being a plate juggler to a trapeze artist as he climbed up to get the figure. Sophie and I were on the staircase holding the ladder, but we both knew that if Rambo did fall he was going to be on his own, as our first priority was going to be the Art Deco figure. Rambo was now doing a passable impersonation of a circus acrobat; he looked like a starfish, with one hand on the ladder and one holding the figure, and one foot on a rung of the ladder and the other out at ninety degrees trying to balance himself.

Eventually we got the figure down onto terra firma and it was clear this was the real McCoy; patina doesn't only relate to wood but other materials as well, and the bronze and ivory of this figure had a depth of colour that left you in no doubt it was real. I would need to do a little homework before coming up with a value, but Mrs Cotswolds was the perfect client. 'I'll leave it to you, dear – I know you'll do your best. Take her with you and put her in a sale when you think it's right.'

We transported the figure back to the saleroom, where my father had come in to help Windy. Rambo carried her in and we discussed where we should put her whilst I did my research. My father's answer to all things security was to tie it up with baler twine and the more twine you could use, the more secure it was. He had been coming in to help on a more regular basis and his presence was evident. There were rolls of carpet tied so tight that you couldn't open them to see the size, condition or colour, and there were sets of golf clubs tied equally as tight, so you couldn't differentiate a three wood from a putter (I played golf and a lot of folk would argue that I couldn't do that anyway).

The Art Deco figure was signed by the artist, who was Demétre Chiparus, and the bronze girl went by the name of Almeria. It was the study of a young lady standing on one leg with the other raised high, both of her arms were raised above her head as she leaned to one side, and she was standing on a marble base. It was definitely of the period. A lot of the modern replicas are made from resin rather than ivory;

ivory has a number of small lines in it whereas resin is completely flat. If you place a piece of known ivory next to resin for comparison the difference is obvious.

I was happy that this was fine, particularly as we had some old photographs of it that Mrs Cotswolds had given us. One last thing I needed to check was the height and I walked over to the shelves to get the figure down to measure it. I went to pick Almeria up and I couldn't move her; it was as if she was glued to the shelf. Then I saw evidence of my father's handi-work: he had tied orange baler twine so tight around the marble base and onto the shelf below that Almeria wouldn't budge. Sophie came in and saw me struggling with it.

'Philip, you need to have a word with your father – every-thing in the saleroom is tied up with baler twine. You can't move for the stuff.' She did have a point.

Come sale day, I was confident Almeria would sell well and the bidding was all on the telephones from London, South Africa and somewhere in Russia. In the end, she was going to be making her way to the home of a London client, who paid £90,000 for it. That was a good price. I had agreed a reserve with Mrs Cotswolds of £30,000; her response being, 'That's fine, dear, whatever you think.'

The chap who bought it had never seen it and relied totally on my descriptions and the photographs we had sent him. It was a scary responsibility, but it did seem to get the results.

'Well, dear, that sold well, didn't it?'

Mrs Cotswolds became a long-time client and I looked forward to my trips to Gloucestershire. I was guaranteed to see good things, but also be the recipient of a proper cup of tea and a slice of Madeira cake.

Chapter 12

Sweet Nothings

At home it was good to relax and take the Worm out for a walk before our evening meal. We hadn't seen Jim Johnson for a while and I was concerned about his welfare, so I thought I'd give him a call before we ate.

'I've got myself a bird and she's really keen.' Whatever Jim lacked, it wasn't confidence. 'I'm going to be off the radar for a bit – she wants some quality time with me.' I told him that might be tough, which went completely over his head. We chatted about how things were going at work and he was happy. Jim was really into his farming and in some ways I was envious of him; I was born into the country way of life, but I didn't ever see it as a career.

As soon as I put the phone down, it rang again and was Rose's father. I settled down by the fire; the Serrell family must have been hiding in a cupboard when the good Lord was dishing out conversation skills, whilst the Hall family could speak for hours about nothing in particular. I prepared myself for a late supper when Rose called out, 'Phil, Daddy would like a word.'

Oh dear, this could mean another crackpot inventor. We got over the first hurdle of exchanging pleasantries before he hit me with the heart of the matter, which was that he had a chap whose company was going into liquidation. I think Rose's father thought I was a cross between a knight in shining armour and the Messiah. Apparently this chap sold sweets – I wasn't sure how my skills as an antique auctioneer qualified me to help a man who sold confectionary, but it was a job.

I thought I would take my father with me and leave him to sort things out. The premises being where they were was ideal for him as it was a good distance from my mother and more importantly was far enough away from Malvern, so that I wouldn't keep popping in to eat the assets.

My father and I made our way to the job; by now he had made up his own auction box of essentials for preparing a sale. It had a screwdriver, the biggest hammer you have ever seen, a ball of baler twine the size of a large beach ball, chalk and enough buff tie-on labels to paper a wall. It was an interesting mix, but not what I would have deemed crucial to lotting up a sale.

We arrived at the address Rose's father had given me and it didn't look much like a sweet shop to me. It was a factory unit on an industrial estate and if it was full of sweets, there must have been tons of them. I pressed the door bell and a chap about thirty years of age appeared.

'You the bloke Mr Hall said would sell me stock?'

As we walked in, it became apparent that there had been a slight misunderstanding. The warehouse was indeed full, but they were suites not sweets – three-piece suites and about two hundred of them.

'Well, this is me suites – if you tell me what you think they'm worth, I'll buy 'em off you an' I can get on with me business.' I wasn't sure we were on the same page here. 'Oh and don't put too much on 'em – they'll have to be cheap,' he joked. I think we both knew that stock in insolvency sales hardly ever made what it cost.

The first thing to do was make a list of all the suites, which my father went off to do; he looked a little down in the mouth at first, as there was nothing for him to use from his new box of tricks. However, the old man was in his element walking round with a clipboard; there were about 188 new three-piece suites which he was making a detailed inventory of.

'OK, how much then?' Our director was a man of few words, but he was short and to the point. I told him I would think about it and come back to him.

That night I called Rose's father and talked the job through with him. Basically, he spelled out that my role was to sell the suites for the most amount of money that I could and also that justice had to be seen to be done. The answer was undoubtedly a sale by auction. Then he threw me a curve ball. 'Philip, there are a few suppliers who haven't been paid for their stock that you'll have to deal with.'

The law at that time was quite complex in respect of goods supplied that had not been paid for, and in layman's terms the supplier was unlikely to be able to reclaim any stock for which he had not been paid.

I telephoned the director the next day to ask him how many of the suites had been paid for. 'None of 'em. That's not really very important – I wanna know how much I can buy 'em for.' He clearly saw the whole situation as a business opportunity rather than a business problem. I pointed out that there was a process to go through.

'I know all about your process; my mate's been bust four times.' I was beginning to think he knew more about it than I did. 'I know they can't have their stuff back. May as well flog it to me – save on costs.'

I asked him for a list of all the suppliers and when I got back to the saleroom, I fired off letters letting them know the situation and that they were unlikely to get their suites returned.

I'm not sure I was cut out for insolvency work. I was getting letters from suppliers threatening me with all sorts of trouble, not least of which was legal action if I didn't arrange to return their unpaid stock. I decided to call Rose's father for more advice.

'Phil, you've made the decision to auction all the stock off. It's the right one to make. Just tell the suppliers and the director that's what's happening. And don't worry!'

I drafted the appropriate letters to the suppliers and decided to drive out with my father and tell the director that we were going to auction. You can only talk to those that want to listen – and this man didn't.

'Why's that old bloke sticking numbers on everything? I thought I was buying it.' I ignored the 'old bloke' bit, though it did make me smile, and told him the plan. 'But I wanna buy it all – who you supposed to be acting for?' I knew the answer to that, but it was clear he didn't. I think this was down to a total lack of understanding rather than anything untoward.

Mr Hall had told me that we should secure the premises and I was wondering how to break this to the director when the task was taken from me. My father broke the news with the subtlety of a sledgehammer. 'I've put some padlocks on the front and back doors – nobody can get in or out now.'

'Bloody stupid, this is! I'm gonna phone that Hall bloke and tell 'im.'

We locked the premises up, much to the annoyance of the director, who demanded a key. My father took a certain amount of pleasure in declining that request; I was beginning to think he was enjoying the confrontation. We made our way back to the saleroom and when we arrived, there was a message waiting for me to call Mr Hall and the director.

I rang my father-in-law first. 'Phil, don't worry, you've done the right thing and you've made the right decisions.' That was some comfort; then came the call from Mr Angry. ''E says it's up to you. Why can't I buy me own stuff back. Bloody scandal, it is.' I pointed out to him that as he hadn't paid for any of it, strictly speaking it wasn't his, and his creditors would not be too happy if I sold it all back to him.

'It's all last season's ranges anyway – I'll give you half what it cost me.' I pointed out to him again that this wasn't the way the job worked. I put the phone down only to be told there was an irate creditor on the other phone wanting the suites back that his company hadn't been paid for. This job was beginning to take over my life. It went on like this for the next week or so, with angry creditors wanting their unpaid stock back and an even angrier director complaining that I wouldn't sell the suites back to him.

In some ways this was the most frustrating, as he seemed to have an inability to understand that my job was to sell the stock for as much as I could get for it – not to knock it out to him for no money at all.

My father went over to the unit on a fairly regular basis to check on the security. On that front I was happy; even if they could cut through the miles of baler twine, they would have to get past the padlocks first. He was proving a master at putting in his expenses claims, too. I had agreed to pay him a mileage rate, though I hadn't banked on him going from Malvern to the warehouse via Aberystwyth.

The sale was fixed for a Monday, which was an unusual day for us to hold a sale as they were normally on Thursdays. Being a superstitious individual, I hoped this wasn't going to bring us bad luck. I met up with Jim Johnson on the Friday before the sale at the Greyhound and he was his usual ebullient self. 'It'll be fine, Phil – everybody wants a new three-piece suite. Anyhow, this new bird I've got is really keen. I mean she would be, wouldn't she?' Some questions didn't need answering.

I was trying to get a bit of comfort from Jim that my sale would go alright, but he was far more interested in telling me how lucky his new girlfriend was. I think I drove Rose round the bend when I got home, as my anxiety reached new levels.

The plan on Monday was for my father to go over early in the morning and open up the premises for the viewing, and I would drive over later to start the sale at 11 a.m. There were only 188 lots, so it would all be over in less than two hours. I didn't expect the Harrods soft-furnishings buyer to be in attendance, but the suites would be good value at somewhere between £200 and £400 each. In an area like this, with lots of new housing estates, I could see there being a good demand.

I was about to leave the saleroom on Monday morning when Windy came rushing up to me. 'Phil, your dad's on the phone . . . says they've had a break-in.' That was all I needed – I rushed to the phone.

'We've had a break-in.' I knew that, but the question was how much had they taken? For one minute I thought my father had said everything. He had.

'Everything. That's what I said . . . they've taken *everything.*'

I jumped in the car and made my way over to the warehouse as quickly as I legally could. When I arrived, my father was talking to a couple of policemen by the main door, whilst outside was a queue of locals all wanting to buy a three-piece suite.

'What's going to happen now – my husband's given me the money for a suite?' was typical of many questions that were directed at me. I walked into the unit and asked my father exactly what they had taken.

'I've told you – everything. Lot, stock and barrel.' I think he thought 'Lot' instead of 'Lock' was vaguely amusing, but not right now.

I could see that someone had broken in at the rear of the unit and every one of my 188 lots had gone. They must have had a fleet of furniture vans here all weekend to clear the place. There was nothing more to do than tell Rose's father what had happened and make my way back to the saleroom. Mr Hall was fairly philosophical and said he would refer it to the insurers.

I think the director was as upset as anybody as he had appeared at the sale and had been hoping to buy as much of the stock back as he could. If nothing else I think he had finally grasped the finer points of the insolvency laws.

There was a lovely man who lived about a mile from the saleroom called Eric. He was passionate about Worcestershire and all things connected to the county. In the snappy dressing department, Eric was not a winner – his usual attire was a blue nylon blazer with a hand-sewn, black Worcestershire badge on it; a red round-neck sweater and a county tie that he wore outside the sweater; grey and filthy nylon trousers; and black slip-on shoes with Velcro straps.

He also had a ten-year-old Ford Fiesta that was smothered in the plastic flag badges of the type you see in the rear window of caravans, with the names of every town in the county that he had visited. The *pièce de résistance*, however, was that somehow Eric had managed to get a badge from Morgan, the Malvern motor car manufacturer, which he had stuck with Araldite onto the bonnet of the trusty Fiesta.

The thing about Eric was that he could paint – and I don't mean walls and ceilings. Constable, Turner, Hockney: he was Malvern's answer to any painter you cared to mention, and very good he was, too. He never intended to deceive anyone; he simply enjoyed painting. He used to put his paintings into the auctions and he was well known around Malvern; in his own way he had a bit of a local following. He was a lovely man.

'Morning, Philip – could you sell my Rembrandt for me, please?' Eric had under his arm a portrait of a bearded man in a modern gilt frame. It was a well-executed copy, but was obviously that; there was no depth to the paint and it was fresh and brand-new. The real tell-tale sign was that it was painted on a rectangular panel of ContiBoard (and Eric told me he had painted it himself!).

In terms of estimate, Eric was happy to put the auctioneer's friend of £80–100 on it without a fixed reserve – so-called because it appeared on many lots in sales and was regarded as a bit of a 'come and buy me' figure. The new saleroom software meant that we could upload images of every lot in the sale so that potential buyers could see the lots online. This auction was typical of most of the sales we were holding, with an interesting selection of lots in most categories, and we were receiving emails from across the world asking for details and images about the sale.

'Philip, you'd better have a look at this.'

Sophie handed me an email about a book in the sale concerning a region in India, written by a traveller in the nineteenth century and including maps and engravings of the region. It wasn't a particularly valuable book, and on the price guides that I had looked at it was worth between £200 and £300, but the email was saying that the sender wished to buy it 'whatever it cost'.

I decided to call them, as I wasn't happy to take an open-ended 'buy it' bid. I had never forgotten an instance many years ago when one of the lots in the sale was an atlas and two interested buyers had independently gone to two members of staff and said, 'Just buy it for me.' The net result was that a £50 atlas had cost the buyer nearly £400 and caused the firm a lot of embarrassment.

I spoke to the sender of the email, the agent for an Indian Prince, whose family owned most of the land described in the book. Apparently they had been looking for a copy for some time and were very keen to buy the one I had in my sale. I suggested that a telephone bid was the sensible option and I was absolutely delighted when he bought it for £310.

'Philip, you'd better have a look at this.'

There was a feeling of déjà vu as Rambo handed me another piece of paper; it was an email from a chap in America who was interested in Eric's painting. Interest was something of an understatement as I read the email. The American had left a bid of just over £26,000. I thought I had better phone him. It was fairly obvious that he thought he might be buying the auction-room sleeper to end them all. I went to some lengths to explain to him that we were very comfortable with the fact that it was a modern copy, but this didn't seem to deter him and he confirmed he wanted us to bid on his behalf.

When an interested party leaves a bid with a firm of auctioneers, there's an unwritten rule that it is treated with respect and that the auctioneer doesn't run the bid up to the maximum. It doesn't always happen that way, but auctioneers who do adhere to that way of doing business will generally get better prices; more people will leave bids, but they will also leave higher ones. Our American Old Master specialist was the successful buyer of Eric's masterpiece for £180.

Now I never expected any financial reward, but I thought the buyer might have said thank you for saving him so much money. I heard nothing at all from him; it was collected on his behalf and I presume his 'Rembrandt' is now hanging on his wall over a 'Sheraton' table with a 'Fabergé' egg on it.

My father was very enthusiastic in helping at the saleroom; throughout his life he had turned his hand to many things, none of which had been hugely successful. He and Windy formed an alliance that was not dissimilar to Laurel and Hardy and I have to say if I wanted to discuss the finer points of eighteenth-century Worcester porcelain, it would have been with Sophie and Rambo rather than the other two. Bearing that in mind, I felt a certain amount of trepidation when my father told me that he had a job for us; I was doubtful it would involve an illustration on the front cover of our next Antique and Fine Art sale catalogue.

'My old mate's got a lorry he wants to sell.'

One of the old man's many guises in his former life was as the owner of two lorries that traded under the banner of

'Peter Serrell Transport'; it was not a threat to Eddie Stobart. I knew that some of these old lorries, provided they were old enough, could be worth a lot of money.

'It's not a new one,' he went on, 'but it's not really vintage either.' So it was just an old lorry then. Against my better judgement, I agreed to put it into one of our general sales and told my father that the vendor could bring it to the saleroom and we would store it pending the auction.

I had forgotten the conversation until I arrived at the saleroom one morning and it had been delivered in my absence. The paintwork was interesting; it was as if a class of naughty nine-year-olds had been given the task of decorating it for a flower-power pop concert. The names of former owners had originally been sign-written and then painted over by subsequent owners, but could still be seen faintly underneath. I knew nothing about lorries, but it looked like a wreck in my eyes; judging by the mileage, it must have done daily trips to the moon and back, and the tyres were on the smooth side of bald.

I walked into the saleroom office, where Sophie, Rambo, Windy and my father were all having a coffee break.

'Have you seen it?' was Sophie's opening gambit. 'I think it's seen better days,' was Rambo's verdict, to which Windy added, 'Haven't we all!'

I asked my father why they didn't park it round the back.

'You're lucky they got it that far, or unlucky depending on your perspective,' observed Sophie. 'They got it to where it is now and the engine died.' She was enjoying this. 'The brakes have seized up, so you're not going to move it anywhere now,' joined in Rambo. 'More like bloody impossible,' chirped Windy, who clearly didn't want to be left out.

My father was obviously wounded by these jibes. 'You

wouldn't be complaining if someone brought in a Worcester vase that was going to make a few hundred quid.' He had a point there, to which Sophie replied, 'Yes, but it looks like someone has just dumped it here. You wouldn't dump Worcester vases.' She had a point as well.

As far as I could see, it was going to have to stay where it was, as we couldn't move it even if we wanted to.

The sale day arrived that included the lorry and whilst it was parked up, it drew more than one 'humorous' remark – 'I've got some scrap at home, can I dump it on the pile outside, Phil?' and 'Didn't know you'd gone into the transport business!'

I was worried if I would even find a buyer for it. The vendor had said to my father, 'I don't want it back,' and I shared his sentiments. There is a very fine line between asset and liability, and in my view the lorry fell into the latter category. What I did know was that auctions always drag folk out of the woodwork and there is a buyer for everything somewhere – all you have to do is find them.

I have mentioned before that various buyers seem to have their own particular dress code or uniform, and buyers of scrap lorries had their own. It was a flat cap at 45 degrees to the head that could have been used to wipe an oily dipstick; a filthy, loud red-check shirt; a pair of dark blue jeans covered in axle grease; and a pair of dealer boots. They all walked around the lorry muttering things about horsepower, pulling power and axle ratios. It seemed a bit academic to me, as the biggest issue would be moving the thing.

From what I could pick up it was a 'breaker' – apparently it was the term for a vehicle that you could take apart and sell for spares. That was fine, as long as they didn't take it apart where it was now parked. The whole business seemed an awful lot of work for a few hundred pounds.

The lorry actually made £400, which delighted my father. 'Two hundred lots of those and you'd have a good sale.' Correct, though I wasn't sure where we would put them all.

The buyer was wearing a scruffy suit and the world's supply of hair oil on a quiff that would have embarrassed Elvis Presley. I wandered over and asked him where he was from and how he was going to get the lorry home.

'Oh, we'll drive her back.' I felt I should point out that might be a problem. 'Don't worry, one of the lads is on his way over in the Land Rover – he could get a stationary engine moving.'

Sure enough, a Land Rover pulled into the saleroom car park driven by a wiry individual who jumped out and without a word started to fiddle about in the engine bay. He got out a battery and some jump leads that would have started an aircraft carrier, but they wouldn't start this lorry. We all stood looking at it.

'We'll have to get Dave over in Bertha.' I was loath to enquire who Dave was, much less Bertha. 'Ar – Dave and Bertha'll soon have 'er out.'

I wandered back into the saleroom office and about an hour had passed when I heard a roar from outside the saleroom. I went out to see the most enormous lorry tractor unit, like the ones the army use to tow tanks. However, that's where the similarity ended – this wasn't painted in a drab army green, but was bright red with *Bertha* written in gold letters on the side. Dave got out and he was nearly as big as his truck. He pulled out from the passenger side a length of chain with links about a foot across; it must have weighed a ton. I decided to stay around and watch the whole performance.

Dave attached the chain to the back of Bertha and to the front of the lorry. He climbed into Bertha, let out the clutch, hit the accelerator and ... nothing. The truck was dragged forward a few yards with the brakes locked before Bertha stalled. Dave got out and surveyed the situation – this was clearly an affront to his manhood and he was in no mood to be defeated. He climbed back into Bertha, revved the engine until you could barely hear yourself think, and dropped the clutch.

Initially nothing moved, but then Bertha shot through the saleroom gates and across the main road. The old lorry on the back reminded me of a slalom water skier being towed by a boat that was going too fast. It swung from side to side completely out of control; we all stood there watching and unable to say a word. The front of the lorry completely demolished one of the brick gateposts at the entrance to the saleroom.

Dave can't have known any of this, because he turned right onto the main road. The effect of him turning right was to swing the old lorry out more and at a greater speed. He only came to a halt after the pendulum at the back of Bertha had written off three parked cars. It was going to be a surprise when their owners came out of the saleroom to drive home. Dave got out of the cab and scratched his head as he looked at the carnage.

'That's a bit of a bugger,' said the wiry Land Rover driver, whilst his boss stood and whistled. One of the car owners happened to wander out, saw his twelve-month-old car and started to cry.

In fairness, the chap's insurance company sorted out all the claims in full and I got a brand-new brick gatepost. Sophie, Windy, Rambo and I were in the office having a coffee a couple of days later, when my father came in.

'The bloke who sold the lorry wants to know if we'd like to have a go at another.'

Nothing was said. We all just got up and walked out.

Chapter 13

The Picture Man

Henry Edwards was a real ducker and diver, as well as being a bodger extraordinaire. He was a working-class man who had come from a council estate in Worcester and had started out in life as a painter and decorator. He was an incredibly hard-working individual – as my father liked to say, he worked twenty-five hours a day because he used to work in his lunch hour.

As time went by, his interest in antiques grew until it got to the point where his painting and decorating was confined to the small timbered cottage he had bought on the outskirts of Malvern. His passion for antiques, however, had grown so much that it had become his full-time career; eighteenth- and nineteenth-century furniture were his thing.

What he did have was a feeling for timber and an ability to turn a sow's ear into a silk purse. He could marry two bits of furniture to look as if they had spent the whole of their lives together, and he had some mystery potion that he used to create instant patina. I used to tell him that if he could market the stuff, he would make a fortune.

In fairness to him, he never misdescribed his creations; he simply let the buyer or auctioneer make up their own mind as to what they were looking at. He was not the most popular amongst the other dealers, who I think saw him as an outsider that hadn't come into the business through the established routes. They may also have been a little afraid of being caught out by one of his creations. He was an interesting character, whom I quite liked.

'Phil, I'm moving from the cottage – I want you to do a sale on the premises. Would you please come over and have a look?' I think Henry had probably done as much as he could to the cottage by way of improvement and it was time for him to move on to another project.

I drove out to see him and it was obvious he had done a first-class job restoring it; the cottage was filled with some lovely pieces of furniture. There was also a range of outbuildings that doubled up as his storeroom and stock workshop. This was going to be a good job.

'Thing is, Phil, they might be good but I don't want those kids doing it,' he said, which I thought was a bit harsh on Sophie and Rambo, who had developed into two good auctioneers. 'So, if you want the job, you have to do it.'

There were about 750 lots and Henry, as ever keen to keep the costs down, said he would do all the sorting and lotting himself; so all I had to do was turn up and sell. The only thing we needed to do now was arrange a date for the sale, which Henry said he would come back to me on.

I arranged to meet Jim at the Greyhound on the way home and we chatted about an upcoming boys' night out that we had planned. I hadn't seen that much of him of late – he was all loved up. 'Phil,' he declared confidently, 'I think she's the one for me.' I wondered how she felt about that.

It was the local cricket club annual dinner three weeks on Friday and Jim and I were going to it. It was the awards dinner; though at the end of it, no one could ever remember who had won what. Whereas I played cricket for them, Jim didn't; not only that, but he didn't know a cricket bat from a tennis racket, though that didn't stop him telling me, and anyone else who would listen, that he could have been a cricketing world beater.

Rose and I lived within walking distance of the club and the local pub where the dinner was to be held, so Jim would stay at our little cottage after the dinner had finished. He was good company but a bad influence, so it was bound to be a boozy do. It was a night we were both looking forward to.

I had started to do a few talks to the local Women's Institutes and they seemed to be going quite well. I think word had spread and a local farmers' group had asked me to speak at their annual dinner. I would have to make sure I was on my 'A game'. The farming fraternity would be harsh judges, but there was the added bonus of a top drawer roast-beef dinner on offer. The talk was booked for the coming Saturday evening, which meant I could spend the Saturday afternoon preparing my talk.

I finished work on the Friday evening and called into the Greyhound, where Jim was holding court. 'Of course, I could have been a really quick bowler if I'd put my mind to it.' That was Jim all over.

I had a quick pint and made my way home to one of Rose's casseroles with dumplings, mashed potatoes and vegetables. After that, and seconds, I was full to busting and sat down to relax when the phone rang. Rose answered it.

'It's a chap from the farmers' group. Wants to know where you are?'

I grabbed the phone in a panic.

'Evening, Philip – just checking that you're on your way.' I'd got the wrong date; it was the Friday night not the

Saturday. 'OK, we'll see you in a while – we've got the biggest Yorkshire pudding in the world for you.'

I shot upstairs, got changed and drove over as quickly as I could, wondering what the hell I was going to talk about.

I arrived just as the bunch of ruddy faced farmers were sitting down to prawn cocktail. 'We'd heard you'd got an appetite, Phil, so we've got a good slab of beef for you,' said the chairman sitting next to me. My trousers felt tight before I got there; after I made the half-hearted attempt to eat the side of a cow that had been cooked for me, I could barely move. Not only that, but there were beads of sweat starting to form on my forehead as I worried about what on earth I was going to say; I would have to rely on some sort of divine inspiration.

They cleared the dinner plates away and plonked a huge dish of jam roly-poly and custard in front of me. I was convinced I was in heart-attack country as I pushed my pudding around the dish, trying to make it look as if I was eating some of it.

'We're all really looking forward to hearing what you've got to say.' Me too, I thought. 'We had a really good speaker last year.' As anyone who has ever done any public speaking will tell you, this is not what you want to hear before you get up to speak; I've always been easily intimidated.

How I got through the next half-hour I will never know. I have vague recollections of telling them that Victoria was a queen who lived in the nineteenth century and similar inspirational facts. I am sure they thought I was a complete idiot. The whole time I felt completely weighed down with Rose's casserole, prawn cocktail, a full-on roast with all the trimmings and a pudding. I was going to need a sedan chair or stretcher party to get me back to my car.

Eventually it was all over and I was able to go home. When Rose asked how it had gone, I'm afraid I ignored her and took myself straight off to bed. I was so full.

Back to work on Monday morning and there was a message waiting for me from Henry with the date he wanted for the auction. It was the Saturday after the cricket club bash on the Friday night. It was a bit of a blow, but I had to do a good job and work comes first, so I would need to have a quiet night with Jim at the club dinner.

Suited and booted, Jim and I made our way to the Greyhound for a quick sharpener before the do; in reality, a quick sharpener turned into three quick sharpeners before we went off to the dinner.

'I'll order some vino collapso,' said Jim, perusing the wine list with the eye of someone who was writing a wine column for the Sunday newspapers. I don't know why he bothered, as we were completely driven by budget and the finest Hungarian red delivered in bulk plastic bottles was our normal tipple; not out of choice, but of necessity.

'Four bottles of the red, please.'

I pointed out to Jim that there were only the two of us drinking, to which he replied we could always come back for another couple later on. We didn't order any more wine; primarily because Jim decided we should have a bottle of port with the cheese, followed by a brandy. 'It'll help the digestion of the cream on that Irish coffee we've had.'

At the end of the night, we quietly rolled our way back to chez Serrell. Rose had sensibly gone to bed, leaving Jim to scour the house for more alcohol. That was the last thing in the world I either wanted or needed but, as we all know, sense and reason go out of the window after a couple of drinks. After what we'd had, they didn't stand a chance.

'I've found these two bottles, Phil – we'll give them a go.' This was now the end. Jim had found bottles of my mother's home-made rhubarb wine, which my father had given us as a Christmas present; mainly because he refused to drink the stuff himself. You could run a car on it and I watched as Jim filled up two half-pint glasses that he had found. It had the consistency of Castrol GTX motor oil, was bright red in colour and had bits floating in it.

I took a sip – you couldn't really taste anything as it ripped the enamel off your teeth – and my lips felt as if they were on fire. Sometimes when you've had too much to drink, the evil spirit takes over and you don't know when to stop. In this particular instance, Jim and I should have stopped about five hours earlier, but we were made of stronger stuff than that and we kept going – and going.

I never actually made it into bed and fell asleep in the chair, whilst Jim was comatose on the floor making noises like a ship in the fog. I woke up with a jolt; my head was aching in a way I had never experienced before and it felt as if someone had welded my lips together. Thankfully, Rambo was picking me up in the morning and I wasn't driving, as I would have melted a breathalyser.

'Jeez, Phil,' croaked Jim. 'What the bloody hell was in that stuff your mother made – kerosene?'

Rose came down and asked us if we'd like a bacon sandwich; I wasn't sure if she was being serious or it was a poor attempt at humour. Either way I declined, feeling pretty queasy, but the mention of food perked Jim up.

'Yes, please, Rose – and a fried egg with mine. Make the yolk runny.'

I vanished to the bathroom and managed to shave and put on a clean shirt before Rambo arrived. He looked a little puzzled when I asked if he could drive on straight roads rather than go round bends; I was feeling nauseous and the head pounding had got worse. I wasn't sure my body would take being moved around too much.

'I think we're going to have a jolly good sale today.' Rambo was trying hard to make conversation with me, as hard as I was trying not be violently ill. How I was going to get through the next ten hours or so was beyond me – this was the hangover from hell.

When we eventually arrived at Henry Edwards' place, I asked Rambo to tell Henry that I was going to have a quiet look around the lots to prepare myself for the sale. In reality, I was going to find a darkened room where I could try and get everything together.

My quest for a bit of peace failed miserably as various prospective buyers wanted to know about lots in the sale; I'm embarrassed to say that I might not have been as helpful as I could have been. The only place where I could find some peace was in one of the portaloos that Henry had hired specially for the auction. The length of time I locked myself in there must have been of some concern for those waiting outside – for any number of reasons.

'Good luck, Phil! Do a good job for me.'

Those were my client's instructions as I climbed onto our makeshift rostrum of four old pallets; I know it wasn't that high, but I began to feel rather dizzy. The first ten or fifteen lots seemed to go well as I got into my stride, but after that things went downhill rapidly. Every time the gavel came down, there was an explosion going off in my head. We had no amplification system, so I was having to shout, which conspired to make everything worse. I did not feel well and was beginning to wish I'd drunk water the night before.

I got to lot 57 and knew I couldn't go on. I also couldn't ask Sophie or Rambo to sell, so for the first and only time in my career, I took a comfort break – or an uncomfortable break. My two loyal assistants looked on with genuine concern as I made my way back to the portaloo. I don't know who Murphy was, but his law was in evidence, for there was a queue a mile long outside the loos. Thankfully, those at the front felt some sympathy.

'We'd better let you go first,' they said, after taking one look at me.

The portaloo was one of those plastic Tardis things that seemed to echo every sound. There is no easy way to say this, but I was violently ill and after I had collected myself together, I opened the door to see the long queue of folks staring at me. No one said a word and they parted like the Red Sea as I made my way, head down, back to the rostrum.

'Christ, you look green!' were the comforting words from Sophie as I took the gavel, followed by a supportive 'Rather' from Rambo.

I'm not sure how I got through the rest of the sale, but I did and I'm told I did a first-class job of it. I have never been so relieved to finish an auction and Henry was delighted.

'Bloody good job, Phil, I'm really pleased – come inside and have a drink.'

At that point I made my way back to the portaloo – vowing never to drink again.

Victorian furniture was selling well at the moment and dining-room furniture was particularly sought after, so I was pleased when a client brought in a set of six chairs for our next sale. I was in a bit of a rush as I was off to see another client, but told Rambo I thought they should make

£300–500 and that I would catalogue them when I got back.

I was due to go and see a lady who had been referred to me by another local firm of auctioneers and had a modern painting to sell. I had looked up the artist – he was a man who painted portraits and landscapes in the middle of the twentieth century – and he made serious money, so I was keen to get it in for sale. As a country auctioneer, it was helpful to have a number of specialists to call upon for advice when the situation arose. This was one of those occasions, so I made the call to the Picture Man.

He and I had been friends for more years than either of us cared to remember and his knowledge was at a different level. Having a photographic memory helped, but it was the range of his subject that was so invaluable. I would back his knowledge from about AD 1200 through to artists from the present day; these attributes had seen him buy paintings for hundreds of pounds and sell them for a figure many times more than what he had paid.

He was a man of few words and when he came into the saleroom to look at watercolours and paintings, his responses were kept to a minimum: 'Rubbish', 'Rubbish', 'Rubbish', and very occasionally, 'That's OK'. The latter usually meant it was worth a few thousand pounds. I very rarely got a 'Good' out of him and anything better than that was reserved for the very best.

We pulled up at the house in question, which was a timber-boarded barn with a large pool in front. It was a sunny day and before I went in, I had a feeling that it would be light, airy and modern inside. The barn was painted in a light pastel green that would have made the National Trust proud. We were greeted by the lady of the house and walked in. It was exactly how I thought it would be: contemporary and with some well-chosen lighting that made it all work. The furniture in there was also very cool.

The lady explained, 'My father was an architect in London and liked to go to exhibitions and galleries.' It was evident they had bought a lot of their collection in the 1950s and 1960s and the building and its contents were like being in a contemporary gallery. 'It was a passion that my mother shared as well.'

As we chatted, she told the Picture Man and me that her parents had bought what they liked, rather than for investment, and supported a number of up-and-coming artist and cabinet makers; some of whom had proved to perform better financially than the stock market.

We made our way to the far wall of the barn where the painting was hung; I have to say it was not to my personal taste. The artist was born shortly before the start of the First World War and died in the late 1970s; if you had to put him into a pigeon hole, he was an abstract painter. I have always had a simplistic view when it comes to art – if you need to explain it to me, do not hang it on my wall. His portraits did look like people, but his landscapes, and this was one, were a series of geometric shapes; mainly squares, rectangles, circles and ovals.

The Picture Man stood there looking at it, while the lady and I were both waiting for him to say something. It was more of an audience really and I was simply hoping he wasn't going to say 'Rubbish'. Eventually, after a long pause, he gave his verdict: 'Good thing'.

This was praise indeed and rarely heard from him. I guessed the painting would have cost a few hundred pounds when bought, which was a lot of money back then. 'Fifteen to twenty thousand pounds,' was the assessment of the oracle. I wasn't surprised, but I simply couldn't see it. Frankly, I would rather have the money than the painting. But I think the Picture Man's estimate was what she expected, because the lady asked me to include it in the next sale and said she would drop it into the saleroom.

It was one of those days that I loved my job; travelling through glorious countryside to a very cool house and coming away with a good lot for the next sale, and I was with the Picture Man, whose knowledge always inspired me. On the way back to the saleroom, he told me about an Old Master painting he had discovered in a minor saleroom in America. It had been estimated at $1000–1500; he had bid $35,000, but had underbid it. The thing about the Picture Man was that whilst he had an appreciation, it was also a business. What impressed me most was that he always backed his judgment; it was something that I admired. The stories he came out with were incredulous and had me sat on the edge of my seat.

Back at the saleroom, I was cataloguing the next sale and picked up one of the set of Victorian dining chairs that had come in. They were mahogany and made in about 1880 with a balloon-style back. With an estimate of £300–500, I thought they should sell quite well. So, I was out of the saleroom when the lady brought in the painting, but I had given Sophie the details and whilst she prepared the receipt, Windy hung it up where it would remain till the auction. It was fairly easy to catalogue, as we had been given the original receipt by the vendor that gave its dimensions and title, which I copied down for the catalogue. For once in my life, the catalogue was all finished and we were ready and waiting to go for the view day.

The level of interest we had received for the painting was good and I was sure it was going to sell – it was only a question of how much it would make. Normally I got a little twitchy when vendors came into the saleroom, but for once I was relaxed when the Painting Lady came in, as I knew we would have a good outcome.

Rambo was proving his spurs in the saleroom, but I knew something was not how it should be whenever he got flustered. This was one of those occasions.

'Er, Philip – the lady would like a word with you about her painting.'

She looked perfectly calm and reasonable, but I could tell something was up.

'Philip,' she said, 'I hope you don't think I'm being picky, but . . .,' I was hoping someone hadn't put a hole in the canvas, 'you've got it hung upside down.'

I apologised profusely and sent her off with Rambo to hang it the right way up, whilst I went off to find Windy and quietly throttle him.

'It's hardly my fault, Phil – if the bloke wants to paint a bloody landscape, it should at least look like a bloody landscape. My grandkids could have done better than that.' There was no point in saying anything. He walked off, muttering, 'Don't know about upside down – could have hung the bloody thing the wrong way round and you wouldn't have known.' I couldn't see Windy writing an article on art appreciation for *Country Life*.

Thankfully, I had listened to the Picture Man rather than Windy, because the purchaser paid £36,000 for the painting; and I have no doubt that he knew the right way to hang it.

The chairs also sold well to a buyer in the room for bang on £400, so we had a good sale. That was until a couple of days later, when I had a phone call from the chair buyer.

'Mr Serrell, I bought the set of six chairs off you in your recent sale – two of them are reproduction and you catalogued them as Victorian. I should like to know your proposals to remedy this?' I told him that I would go out to his house that afternoon to look at them.

When I got there, the atmosphere was decidedly frosty.

'Mr Serrell, I regard this as a serious breach of your duty of care.'

This was a good start, as I hadn't even looked at them yet, but when I did I could see that he was absolutely right and two of them were reproduction. I had only picked up two of the old ones when I catalogued them and assumed they were all old. The new ones didn't have the depth of colour they should have done and were significantly lighter in weight than the old ones.

'I demand to know what you intend to do about this.'

It was quite simple – I had made a mistake, which I told him. I pointed out that the reserve was £300 and as he had paid £400, there must have been an underbidder. On that basis, I had made a mistake and was happy to either refund his money in full or he could pay £200 for them and I would make up the other £200 to the vendor.

'I should like my money back, please.'

I told him this was not a problem, and I would arrange for Big Nige to come around and collect the chairs and give him a cheque to refund the purchase price.

'I'm not prepared to take your cheque – I want cash.'

I have to say I was more than a little put out by this, but arranged for Big Nige to collect the chairs and hand the man a brown envelope full of cash. I was pretty angry that he couldn't accept I had made a mistake, which I had acknowledged and tried to rectify to his satisfaction.

I thought that was the end of the matter, but I was still smarting when about a week later I had a letter from the man's lawyers, pointing out my responsibility and their concern that I may have been trying to deceive their client. I'm afraid this had the effect of lighting the blue touch paper with me and I called the man and his lawyers to tell them both exactly what I thought.

Not really very professional of me, but it did make me feel a whole load better.

Chapter 14

Full Circle

A lot of the saleroom business was based on deceased estates and clearing their properties. You never knew what you were going get; you could walk into a house and find wonderful objects or try to make the best of a bad job, clearing whatever might be saleable and disposing of the remaining contents.

I had a call to prepare a valuation for inheritance tax purposes and clear a property of a gentleman who lived about two miles from the saleroom in Malvern. The instructions came from a firm of lawyers in the town, and I had to go to their offices to collect the keys so that I could carry out my inspection.

I pulled up outside the bungalow and walked up the garden path; the first thing I noticed was that all the curtains were closed. I walked in and put on the hall light and saw that the doors leading off the hall were all shut, which made the bungalow feel quite eerie. My usual plan when doing such a valuation was to have a walk around the whole property first, to see what the job entailed and to check roughly what was in each room. It was a common occurrence to find a set of chairs spread throughout a property, so I always wanted to get my bearings first and try to ascertain what was where.

The first door on the left was a bedroom and a quick glance revealed there was little of any significance in there. You would never expect to find the best lots in the bedroom, but it could sometimes be an indicator as to what you might find elsewhere. Through the darkened room I could see that this house was a shrine to the god of flat-pack, chipboard furniture; the white stuff that was held together by a paper-thin veneer. Having assembled it and put it where you wanted, if you dared to move it, the whole thing fell apart in a pile of sawdust. Not only that, but you would never be able to put it back together again.

I walked into the next room past two modern wing armchairs with their backs to me; like in my parents' house, the chairs were arranged around the fire to ensure the sitters benefited from the maximum warmth when it was lit. As I walked to pull open the curtains, I felt a little spooked; I have said it before, but I suffer from imagination overdrive and somehow it is always worse in the dark. Then I heard a voice.

'Sorry, I didn't expect anyone to be here.'

I nearly jumped out of my skin and cried, 'Bugger me!' I apologised quickly for the expletive that had escaped involuntarily from my mouth.

The voice in the dark came from one of the chairs with its back to me, and probably put me as close to a heart attack as I've ever been. In the light, I could see the outline of a man sitting in the chair.

'I must have shocked you. He was my brother.'

The voice went on to explain that he was paying a last visit to the family home before it was emptied, and I think I gave him as big a shock as he gave me. I felt sorry for him; he and his brother had never married and were the last of the line.

We chatted and he told me that the only thing of any value was a mahogany longcase – or grandfather – clock that his brother had bought at the local auction room. As we walked up to the clock, it did look a little familiar; it was a clock I had sold about four years ago.

The movement was brass-faced and in a mahogany hood. Longcase clocks run for either thirty hours or eight days and the latter are more valuable, as they don't need to be wound up so often. The trunk or the case of the clock forms one part, the face and the movement sit on top of the case, and the hood fits around the movement. The face and movement had not started out life with the case and the hood, and were what is known as a marriage.

The brother was right – it was the only thing worth a shilling in the house. I finalised the valuation and agreed with the brother and the lawyer that the only thing we would take would be the longcase clock.

The clock came into the saleroom and having catalogued it, the next task was to photograph it. I'm not sure if this was how the major London salerooms did it, but we took a white sheet as a backdrop outside and did all our shots in natural light. Windy and Rambo held the sheet, whilst Sophie took the photo – I had the Steven Spielberg role directing operations.

All was going wonderfully well until a gust of wind caught the sheet; initially it looked like Windy was going hang gliding over the Malvern Hills. The clock started to wobble and I could see it was going to land on the gravelled saleroom car park. Never fear, Rambo is here, I thought, as my young colleague leapt forward. That was my mistake.

Instead of catching the clock, he grabbed Windy, who was about to go base over apex. I watched in horror as the clock case hit the ground and smashed to pieces; luckily the face and movement went unscathed.

'That's made a bloody mess of that,' said one of them, or it may have been all three of them in chorus. I dispatched Sophie to get a bag, Rambo to get a broom and Windy to get a shovel, so we could gather up as many of the bits as we could.

'What the 'ell are you going to do with this lot?' was Windy's not unnatural question. I told him I knew a local restorer who could work wonders with wood. 'Restorer? You'll need a bloody magician to sort this lot out!' You could always rely on Windy to sum up the situation, as we stood staring at a bag full of gravel with bits of wood scattered in it.

My restorer man did the most amazing job and put the whole lot back together so that you would have struggled to know it had ever been damaged. It was a costly exercise, but was something I had to do as we had damaged it; the final bill came to £300. On sale day, the clock sold to a dealer from Wales who specialised in longcase clocks – the irony of the whole situation was that he gave exactly £300 for it.

Having bought it, he started to dismantle the clock by taking the hood off the case and then he removed the works. He was walking out to his car with the face and movement under his arm, when he turned and said, 'Phil, can you shove the case and hood in your next sale – no reserve? I only wanted the face and movement. I got a better case for them back home.'

My experience of pianos has never been that great – and grand pianos can present even bigger problems. As with most things in the antique world, there are gold-chip manufacturers that will always do well and in the piano world these are

Bechstein and Steinway. So when Rambo told me that a lady had been on the telephone with a grand piano to sell, my first question was who made it.

'Er – well, I haven't ascertained that yet awhile.' I politely suggested that he should find that out as soon as possible. 'Righto, should I ask her?' I couldn't think of any other way of finding out. 'Excellent, then I'll give her a call.'

I'm glad we got all that sorted out.

Rambo made an appointment to go and see the good lady, and whilst he was out tinkling this lady's ivories, Sophie and I had an appointment to go and prepare a valuation for inheritance tax for the contents of an apartment. The flat in question was the home of a retired businessman and was in the stable block of a large country house.

We drove up the sweeping driveway of an eighteenth-century mansion and introduced ourselves to the agent, whom we were meeting on site, and he gave us the keys to inspect the apartment. As we walked across the courtyard at the rear of the house, I was hopeful that we would see some interesting lots, irrespective of whether they would be sold or not. I opened the door of the stable block and we made our way to the first-floor apartment, but having seen the calibre of prints on the staircase, I did not hold out great hope for finding a rare gem. This was confirmed during our inspection of the apartment.

'Didn't have much, did he?' observed my young colleague. Sophie prepared the bulk of the report and the only things of real value were an eighteenth-century cork work panel, a good period cutlery box, a very ornate silver-plated candelabrum (the difference between a candelabrum and a candelabra is that there's always two in a bra – or that's how I remembered it), and a Derby bough pot. None of these were worth a king's ransom and probably all less than a thousand pounds each. We made our way back across the courtyard and returned the keys to the agent before returning to the saleroom.

'How'd you get on, Rambo – going to sell it to Elton John?' was Sophie's greeting to her young colleague on his return from the piano lady.

'Actually, I think it's a good thing,' he responded, 'and all been fully restored too.' I was a little worried when he told me he had told the lady it might make £300–500 and Sophie's view reinforced this. 'Bloody hell, Rambo, I don't know about selling it to Elton John. D'you reckon he played it?'

The thing that I have always loved about Sophie is that she never soft-soaps her opinion; she normally lets you have it right between the eyes wrapped up in a house brick. Rambo became a little defensive.

'It has been fully restored, and we have all the paperwork.'

'Elton John write that too?' There was no backing off with Sophie once she'd seen a chink; it was very much a case of don't hit a man when he's down – kick him, it's easier.

Rambo had already organised Big Nige to go and collect the piano, so we were committed to putting it in a sale – and to it making the reserve of £300, otherwise it wouldn't cover the haulage costs.

I spoke to the lawyers and having sent them my report of the businessman's apartment, discussed what to do with the contents. The four better bits that Sophie and I found in the apartment had been specifically left to beneficiaries, so the solicitor asked me to arrange the delivery of them, and then to clear the remaining contents. I made another appointment to meet the agent at the stable block to gain access and to let him know what we were planning to do. Sophie was busy in the saleroom, so this would be a solo trip.

'Good morning, Philip. Let me open up for you.' The agent and I made our way upstairs and I showed him around and told him we would be clearing everything except the four items that were on the dining room table, as these were the specific bequests. As we walked into the dining room, I could sense a sudden change in atmosphere.

'Embarrassing this, Philip.' I wasn't sure what he was talking about, but I guessed I was about to find out. 'If those items on the table are the ones you refer to as specific bequests, I am afraid they belong to the main house.'

It transpired that our deceased client had asked the estate if he could store some of his things in the cellars of the main house. Whilst he was taking his clutter down there, he had seized the opportunity of taking these four bits from another part of the cellar, where they were in storage from the big house. Our opportunist businessman had made specific bequests to friends and family of items that he didn't actually own.

I called in at the solicitor's on the way back and told him the situation; in a perverse way, we both admired the brass neck of our deceased client. I thought it best to let the lawyer tell the beneficiaries they were getting nothing.

Back in the saleroom, the piano had been delivered by Big Nige; there was no doubting it looked in good order. The case was in rich burr walnut. The Victorians often used a sponge and dark ink to 'improve' the figuring of the burrs on veneers used in cabinet making, but this was as the good Lord intended it, without any such embellishment at all.

'I've got the restoration costs the lady spent on the move-ment – it was done about six months ago.' Rambo was happy and I think looking forward to watching Sophie and I eat our words. 'I think it'll sell, and do rather well at that too.'

Sophie and I still didn't share his confidence. Come the day of the sale, we decided that he could sell the piano; this was no grand gesture on our part, but more a case of neither of us wanting to die with it. He did indeed prove us wrong, when a local doctor bought it for £300 – bang on the reserve. 'I had a feeling it would sell. I knew the restoration was key, it's all about backing your judgement when you're on the rostrum.'

I didn't say anything and Sophie looked skyward, but Rambo was going to make sure we hadn't heard the last of it. He christened himself 'The Piano Man' and even recorded the Billy Joel song, which he insisted on playing whenever Sophie and I were around. This was all very painful.

It continued for about two weeks until I came back into the saleroom from an appointment to be greeted with, 'Er, Philip ... there's perhaps an issue ... the chap who bought the piano, er ... might be a problem.' You always knew when there was a problem with Rambo – he had an inability to compose a sentence. It appeared that the doctor who bought the piano had asked a piano tuner and expert to have a look at it. The long and the short of it was that the soundboard in the piano was cracked and far from being restored, it was in an unplayable condition.

It was unfair to leave this in Rambo's lap to deal with, so I called the purchaser and asked him to post us a copy of the report that he had. A couple of days later it was waiting on my desk when I got to the saleroom. I thought I would ask 'The Piano Man' to go through it with me, and asked him to get the original paperwork we had from the seller for the restoration work that had been done.

'Well, I must say this makes jolly interesting reading.' Knowing Rambo's reading habits, he might well have been deadly serious, but I asked him why. 'Well, it's the same chap.'

I wasn't sure what he meant so I took the file off him – the man who had restored it for the seller and the chap who had prepared the report for the buyer were one and the same.

I thought it was best if we took a step backwards and I arranged for the buyer and seller to meet with the restorer and sort it out amongst themselves. I'm not sure how it was resolved, but seemingly it was to the satisfaction of all parties. The one good thing to come out of the whole saga was that Billy Joel's 'Piano Man' was no longer on the saleroom playlist.

I popped in to see Mr Rayer fairly regularly and was rather concerned that time was taking its toll on him. His two daughters and son were looking after him and I was in close contact with them, but his health was beginning to bother me. In some ways, I was closer to him than I was my own family; he was a huge part of my personal as well as my professional life. But I suppose none of us can stop the march of time.

Settlebanks was the Rayer family home and had been since Adam was a lad. It overlooked the racecourse in Worcester and had six acres of land – smack bang in the middle of the city.

One of my fondest memories of the house was soon after I had started working for Mr Rayer, when he asked me if I would like some pears. I love pears, so it didn't take me long to reply in the affirmative.

'Call in on the way home and there'll be some for you.'

I'd spent the afternoon on some errand for him that undoubtedly involved counting hop poles, or some other hugely important task, and arrived at Settlebanks at about 6.30 p.m., to be greeted with, 'Hello, Philip – what brings you here?'

This unnerved me a little, though I was to learn later on in my career that this was about par for the course. I reminded him about the pears.

'Well, that's good. There's the ladder, there's the tree and there's a basket in the shed. Whilst you're up there, pick me some as well, please.'

Today was another occasion I was called there, but this time I was not going to be asked to pick pears. 'Philip, I think I've made the decision to move – this old place is all a bit of a barn for me now.'

I was probably more upset than he was; I had seen him age recently and was beginning to worry about his health. Mr Rayer always seemed to take everything in his stride and I concluded that if you had been shot at in the war and nearly died, then other problems that life threw at you were not that great. I had thought he was indestructible.

I'm not sure of the exact date the first Rayers moved into Settlebanks, but I doubt any of them had ever thrown anything away. The house was, at best, somewhat tired and previous generations had contributed to the general state of the place – none more so than the present incumbent.

In auction terms, the house was very much 'af' or as found. Walking around you were as likely to come across a roll of rusting pig wire as a Georgian side table – and this could be in one of the outbuildings or in the house itself. Mr Rayer, as well as being an auctioneer, had made a career of buying utter tat from the auctions and most of it had found its way here.

He had an interesting view on the auctions he conducted – if a lot wasn't selling, he would buy it; there was a flaw in this, for if it wasn't selling it was probably because it wasn't worth anything. He had gathered together a remarkable collection in and around the house of utterly unsaleable rubbish.

'Philip, could you please get Nigel to take what I'm going to keep up to the new place. You can do what you like with the rest of it.'

The tricky part was getting him to leave most of it behind. The new home was a Victorian villa on the south side of the city – I had been there with Mr Rayer and it was definitely a matter of squeezing a quart into a pint pot. I knew he would struggle to leave things behind and value would have no part in the decision-making process. There was no doubt the best way to sort this job was to keep the client as far out of the way as possible.

Mr Rayer had enlisted Windy to help him label up the items he was taking with him and eventually, after they had sorted it all out and Big Nige had got Mr Rayer ensconced in his new home, it was time to tackle the remaining contents. The vast majority of the furniture had seen better days and we moved it to the saleroom and sold it at the first opportunity. Nothing made amazing money, but it all sold and provided a fantastic opportunity for the local restorers to hone their skills.

Some of the chests of drawers and tables made subsequent reappearances at the saleroom once all the faults and wrinkles had been ironed out by their new owners. The strange thing was that many of the lots made more in an unrestored condition than after restoration; a lot of buyers look at projects through rose-tinted spectacles and the finished article can often turn out not the way it was hoped.

The smaller items in the house were nothing much to write home about; *objets d'art* didn't feature large in the Rayer household, but there were a number of prints and general ephemera that you would expect from a house and family that had been in the city as long as they had. There was a huge collection of dodgy hats, coats and sticks in the hallway – a lot of them antiques in their own right.

It involved a fair amount of sorting of the smaller lots, which I left to Sophie and Rambo. There was a distinct division of labour in the saleroom; anything remotely to do with antiques or art was left to those two, 'the kids', whilst anything that required miles of baler twine or piling things into boxes was left in the capable hands of my father and Windy.

''Ere, Phil – there's some of them kilner jars 'ere. Didn't we get twenty five quid for the last lot?' These were the last lot – in fact they still had the old lot number on them from when Mr Rayer bought them from 'Old Mother Gubbins'; and given that he was the only bidder last time, I couldn't see them doing very well this time.

The kids were sorting through a huge bundle of walking sticks when Sophie called me over. 'Have a look at this – I think it might be a good thing.' She passed me a strange-looking, stick-like object about three to three and half feet in length and shaped like a hockey or a shinty stick. The handle part was hatched, I presume to give grip; there were also some notches down the shaft, and one side of the head was carved with a criss-cross decoration. The business end was shaped like a big knife or cleaver, and if you had caught this on the side of someone's head, it would have done serious damage.

Sophie said she would do some research on it, but before she could get up to move, Rambo chipped in, 'I think you'd better have a look at this, too.' He passed me what looked to all intents and purposes like a walking stick; however, on closer inspection the walking stick was a shotgun. There was a trigger concealed in the handle of the stick and below that, the shaft twisted so you could load a cartridge. He had even found a cut-out stock that screwed into the handle. It was all very *Day of the Jackal* type stuff.

Whilst I was sure we could sell the tribal club, and get good money for it – I was equally positive we couldn't sell the gun. I gave Mr Rayer a call. Firstly he had no idea where the tribal club had come from, but thought he may have bought it by accident at a sale – and the walking stick shotgun had always been in the house, but he had probably bought it in a job lot of sticks. 'I used it as bird scarer to keep them off the raspberries in the summer.'

Looking at it, I was surprised he hadn't blown his arm off; it looked a lethal contraption and I told Mr Rayer I thought the best thing to do was to hand it in to the police station. Thankfully he agreed with me and that's what we did with it. I don't think he had any idea that the club was even a club – to him it was probably a 'gubbins' or a 'doings'.

Sophie told me a few days later that she thought it was from the Pacific Islands and probably Polynesian, whilst the carving meant it belonged to a royal or elder and the notches referred to the number of kills the owner had with it. Mr Rayer's club would have been used to split someone's skull open before they were dispatched to the cooking pot. She then went on to show me photographs she had found of cannibal flesh-eating forks, which looked very similar to the small forks that matched a garden trowel – worryingly, I think she was quite enjoying all this macabre stuff.

I have always been fascinated as to how things from far-off lands found their way into rural England – how does a Polynesian club find its way to a house in Worcester? The other thing that intrigued me about items such as the club is the length of time it had gone totally unrecognised in someone's home; in this case, in a stick stand in the hall. In auction terms it was a sleeper; waiting to be woken.

We now knew what it was – the next question was how much it might be worth. I could guess that Mr Rayer's view would be, 'It'll make what it's worth,' but I wanted to have more of a clue than that before we sold it. Sophie was a top auctioneer, but was also developing into a good researcher and I had no doubt she would come back with the answer.

In the meantime, I went up to see how Mr Rayer was settling in at his new home. He had moved in about three weeks earlier and had managed to turn his new house into a mini Settlebanks with stuff everywhere. He had a ordered a new garden shed and had it fitted with shelves, which now housed the Rayer library of horribly out-of-date auctioneering reference books; there was even a book on silver hallmarks that ended at 1928. Inside the house you couldn't see the walls for prints of Worcester, the racecourse and county scenes – there was no need for wallpaper.

He had bought a modern swivel office armchair and was ensconced in it as though he was at mission control. We sat and chatted and he appeared quite happy in his new environment; I told him I was excited about the club that Sophie had identified and wasn't surprised that it raised little interest in him. Like many people in this situation, he had left his old life behind him and all the goods and chattels that went with it.

When I returned to the saleroom, Sophie had done a little more research and thought the club should have a sales estimate of around £2,000–3,000. When adverts and photographs hit the trade papers, we received a large number of enquiries from across the world and three telephone lines were booked before the auction. A continental bidder was successful, with the club making £7,000.

Apparently Sophie had been spot on with her valuation and the estimate was seen to be about right, but the club had a premium because of the clarity of the carving, its original colour and patination – certainly Mr Rayer would never have polished it – and because it was thought to have belonged to a particular member of a royal family.

I called in at Mr Rayer's to tell him that the club had done really well; he seemed more interested in another lot in the sale.

'What did those kilner jars make, Philip?'

I told him that he'd got his money back – they had made twenty-five pounds.

'That's good, Philip. Well done!'

What I didn't tell him was that I had bought them; not only that, but no one else had bid.

The wheel had turned full circle.

Acknowledgements

My thanks to all at Hodder & Stoughton, especially Rupert and Cameron. I'd also like to thank all the people on both sides of the television cameras who've put up with me trying to be a TV presenter – and all the viewers who've been kind enough to say I haven't done a terrible job of it.

An invitation from the publisher

Join us at www.hodder.co.uk, or follow us
on Twitter @hodderbooks to be a part of
our community of people who love the very
best in books and reading.

Whether you want to discover more about a book
or an author, watch trailers and interviews, have the
chance to win early limited editions, or simply browse
our expert readers' selection of the very best books,
we think you'll find what you're looking for.

And if you don't, that's the place to tell us what's missing.

We love what we do, and we'd love you to be a part of it.

www.hodder.co.uk

@hodderbooks

HodderBooks

HodderBooks